PETER DRUCKER'S
SYSTEM OF MANAGEMENT IN A BUSINESS ENVIRONMENT

Dr. Luther C. Guynes, Ph.D.

PETER DRUCKER'S
SYSTEM OF MANAGEMENT IN A BUSINESS ENVIRONMENT

By One of Peter Drucker's First Students:
Dr. Luther Guynes, Ph.D.

PYRAMID PRESS

Copyright © 2019 by Dr. Luther Guynes, Ph.D.

All rights reserved. No part of this book, in part or in whole, may be reproduced, transmitted, or utilized, in any form or by any means, electronic or mechanical, including photocopying, recording, or by any information storage and retrieval system, without permission in writing from the publisher, except for brief quotations in critical articles, books and reviews.

ISBN: 13: 978-0-9968935-5-8
ISBN: 10: 0-9968935-5-5

First Pyramid Press Edition 2019

Graphs and Chapter Summary Art by Sheila Guynes

The paper used in this publication meets the minimum requirements of the American National Standard for Permanence of Paper for Printed Library Materials Z39.48-1984.

Printed in U.S.A.

PYRAMID PRESS
9550 South Eastern Avenue • Suite 253
Las Vegas, NV 89123 U.S.A.
contact@pyramidpress.net

SPECIAL ACKNOWLEDGEMENT OF DR. PETER F. DRUCKER

I extend my deepest gratitude to Dr. Peter F. Drucker for all he taught me over the years. I was fortunate to study under Dr. Drucker's guidance for both my Master's and Doctorate degrees. He was my professor, mentor and friend for over two decades. The knowledge and wisdom Dr. Drucker imparted to me has been both a great help and support throughout my life and career.

One of the most important lessons learned from Dr. Drucker was the implementation of efficiency and effectiveness, and the importance of learning to tell the difference between the two. In addition, I learned the significance that Management is designed to improve self; improve beyond self, and encourage the same manner of improvement in others.

Dr. Drucker influenced and instilled in me diverse skills including the efficiency of speech; how to effectively present arguments for or against a concept or issue, the psychology of learning, how to successfully motivate others, to name a few. In the area of consulting, one of the highlights I remember among many concepts for successful mangers is the belief that with self-control and self-management, one will soar to optimum peaks. Dr. Drucker stressed to me that the importance of working from your strengths and the importance of honesty with oneself when doing so. I also learned about Trust and that Trust requires transparency in personal and business relationships. Trust is the biggest issue impacting work performance as it leads to a heightened sense of conviction and belief.

Dr. Drucker taught me that using feedback is an important key in achieving expertise in talent, and using it to determine your strength to achieve an objective or goal. I recall attending many fireside chats with him and appreciate the support and encouragement he offered then, and throughout the many years.

Moreover, I am honored I was able to become his friend as well as given the opportunity to meet and interact with his family. I cherish the luncheons we shared at his favorite restaurant, and the many invites to join him for dinner at his home.

I remain grateful for the opportunity to share life and time with such a great man. He will forever remain a major contributor of my success and achievements.

                Respectfully yours, Dr. Luther C. Guynes, Ph.D.

Very Special Thanks to DR. MICHAEL MILLER, PH.D., M.Ed., M.S.

I want to thank Dr. Miller for his guidance, assistance, and help in the processing and production of this book. Dr. Miller's vision and insightfulness helped make the book a reality. I also really appreciate him writing the introduction for this. His insight, wisdom and wit are treasures I forever value.

Special Thanks to Those Who Worked on the Book

I especially want to thank the publishing team for their invaluable help and inspiration in the editing and production of this book.

Katherine Morales

Verta Guynes

Kimalica Guynes

Carey Guynes

Sheila Guynes

Zevart Sarkesian

Heidi Ross-Balderama

Appreciation and Thanks for the Drucker Archive Team

I also wish to thank the achieve team for their expertise, knowledge and support for providing relevant content for the book.

Bridget Lawlor

The Drucker Institute

Joan D. Winstein

I want to thank God most of all, because without Him the book would not be possible.

Thank you to all who have contributed in this great work.

DR. LUTHER GUYNES, PH.D.

Dr. Luther C Guynes, Ph.D., began his career in academia at San Bernardino Valley College, Cal Poly Pomona University, and Claremont Graduate University.

He dedicated over forty-five years to higher education as a Professor, Administrative Assistant to the Dean of Business, Assistant to the President, Management Consultant, Department Chair, Dean, Vice President Consultant to Regional Chancellor at National University and President. He has served as Administrative Dean at Los Angeles City College, LA Trade Tech College, Los Angeles Southwest College and Academic Dean at National University. He is the President of the University of Los Angeles College of the Divinity. He also served in the U.S. Marine Corps and was awarded the distinguished Meritorious Mast Award for outstanding service.

Dr. Guynes has extensive experience in the electronics industry starting as an Engineer Checker for Deutsch Electronics in Banning, CA, and Senior Mechanical Design Engineer at TRW Systems in San Bernardino, CA.

He was also the founder and President of Management Systems & Technology, Inc., a technology systems engineering and logistics management consulting firm that provided services to industrial and diverse corporate entities. Services included technical reviews and analysis in diagnosing and implementing systems dynamics, control engineering, algorithmic optimization, computer modeling, application software systems engineering, technical training programs and business logistics.

As a lecturer, Dr. Guynes has made presentations on a variety of subjects ranging from engineering, financial and management-related topics at seminars and conferences at institutions, including Claremont Graduate University, Los Angeles City College, and the Business Department of California Polytechnic University, TRW Systems and Deutsch Electronics.

Dr. Guynes received his bachelor's degree in Business Administration and Industrial Engineering from California State Polytechnic University, Pomona. Under the mentorship of Dr. Peter Ferdinand Drucker, he earned his Master's Degree in Economics and Business Statistics and his Ph.D. in Government Finance and Public Administration from Claremont Graduate University, Claremont, California.

Dr. Peter Drucker considered Dr. Guynes an outstanding student, gifted cooperative colleague and an esteemed professional. Dr. Peter Drucker describes Dr. Guynes as follows:

"Luther C. Guynes, who finished both his Master's work and his Ph.D. work under me, is probably the best administrator I have taught. He has the necessary compassion combined with the necessary toughness. He has insight into people, and yet is task-focused. He is tactful, firm, pleasant and determined. He has that rare gift of making an organization work for him. Altogether, he is one of the few "naturals" in administration I have met, I consider him qualified for any administrative position in higher education, in government service or in business enterprises."

They maintained a meaningful relationship for over twenty-five years until Dr. Drucker's death in November 2005. Dr. Guynes is widely recognized for his expertise in strategic and systems management, organizational development, domestic and international economics, as well as statistics, economics and quantitative analysis.

Over his extensive career, he has received innumerable honors including the Chancellor's Award and several outstanding professor awards as well. Among his professional affiliations, he has been a member of the American Management Association, the International Business Fraternity, and the Kiwanis organization.

Dr. Guynes enjoys playing chess, reading, concerts, discussing philosophy, government, and the economy. He is a loving and devoted father to his six children, nine grandchildren, and four great-grandchildren.

INTRODUCTION

By Dr. Michael Miller, Ph.D., M.Ed., M.S.

"Your first and foremost job as a leader is to take charge of your own energy and then help to orchestrate the energy of those around you."
–Peter F. Drucker

Basically, the history of modern business management can be thought of in two time periods: *before* Peter Drucker and *after* Peter Drucker. It may still be premature to consider such a timeframe; he was, after all, a leader, an advisor and a professor for more than five decades. That is an especially long period for someone to set the pace for so many influential and preeminent ideas. Drucker's innovations in management cover so many broad aspects of business that it can be easy to imagine taking his contributions as a given. Many people, including those who hold a wide range of positions, may not be familiar with Professor Drucker, but they have him to thank for their ways and means of employment.

Drucker was probably the most influential voice in business management in the history of American industry. He created several schools of thought, which are often taken for granted. His ubiquity in the processes of nearly every effective American company or organization is a testament to his greatness. But what made Drucker so respected, and why have so many business leaders been inclined to write books about him and his ideas? The reason for Drucker's success is that he focused on workers as people, and he was able to draw on the distinct psychologies of the executives, the managers and the floor team, while witnessing and comprehending the significant links between the three worker tiers and so finding a way for each level to work together optimally toward a common goal.

Drucker's books have been published many times over the years, and it is hard to find an MBA graduate who is not familiar with Drucker's approach to business management. Many self-made executives and entrepreneurs apply his methods without even being aware of it. Even sports figures like Bill Belichick and Robert Kraft, owner of the recent *Super Bowl LIII* champions, New England Patriots, applies Drucker's philosophies to great success. In fact, whenever you see someone succeeding at the highest levels, they are more than likely benefitting from Drucker's philosophies, as many self-help books take their cues from his early work on self-assessment and self-awareness. His influence permeates all forms of media. He established the Drucker Archives at Claremont Graduate University in 1999; the Archives became the Drucker Institute in 2006. In 2002, when Drucker retired from the classroom, he was 92. He continued consulting businesses and nonprofit organizations well into his nineties.

In the late 1950s, he introduced the concept of the knowledge worker, and it introduced an entire class of business management that recognized that the majority of workers not on an assembly line were skilled laborers, and that skill came with vast knowledge, which benefits the companies that best utilize their resources. Conventional thinking prior to Drucker focused primarily on the needs of the top executives who subordinated other concerns to trickle down, as if ordained by some higher law of nature. Drucker's philosophies inverted that concept of business thinking so the lower tiers might achieve higher levels of performance, and the top executives might follow suit, since they would be freed up to focus on driving the big ideas to innovate and steer the company to success.

Drucker was the first business philosopher to focus on the power of community in the office. He recognized the power of friendly familiarity, and how even those who didn't get along while working side-by-side would still fondly reminisce after periods of separation from the workplace. Especially for start-ups, the power of community is vital in the modern work culture, because startups routinely have less money available to pay their workers. In this way, for example, they might take advantage of characteristically inexpensive community moments such as Pizza Fridays or Bagel Mondays–and startups have made inroads throughout the country. They present moments when young employees discuss their previous weekend events, or some upcoming weekend getaway. It is this community that bonds together a workforce as a *de facto* family, which Drucker recognized decades ago and which could improve American workplaces and the bottom line.

At his core, Drucker was a teacher. He began teaching in the late 1930s and continued all the way into the 21st century – from his college lectures and his decades working as a popular professor on campuses like Bennington College, New York University to, of course, his later years at Claremont Graduate Institute, where the business management school continues to honor Drucker's name since his passing and where his archives are preserved for future generations.

As the father of the modern style of business management, he was much sought after by the world's top general managers and top executives. He would meet with important business leaders, and they would block out hours of their day just to allow the ultimate set of discerning eyes and ears to help capitalize on the untapped potential of their organizations. Whether it was a college student or the Chairman of a blue-chip American corporation like General Electric or Ford, he would ask the same direct questions:

"Who is your customer?"
"What is your mission?"
"What does your customer value?"
"What are your results?"
"If you were just starting out, would you enter this field?"
"What are you great at?"

Often his trademark concise questions would cut straight to the core of a business. There are instances when leaders met with Drucker for an afternoon and re-thought some company policy, and immediately made some seismic, shapeshifting changes. It might have been General Electric's Jack Welch taking a pledge to cease making products in which the company doesn't have one of the top two market shares or inspiring the *Los Angeles Times* to change their approach to covering their city in ways that would better resonate with their dwindling subscribers rolls. Drucker's critiques mattered to some of the most important business leaders in the world, and when he provided his expert set of eyes and ears to their executive suites, he expected and often demanded that he see those he counseled turn their words into positive action.

Drucker was an innovator in business and business management because he focused more on the people working and less on the crunching of numbers. He took a scientist's approach to business, and, as a result, improved business management, sharpened executives' awareness to become more effective, and counseled companies to be more responsive to the value of lower level employees. For more than a half century, recordings he made were hoarded by management students around the globe, and his books have been absolute required readings for business students and top business executives.

Innovation from human resources to management to departments handling actual innovation bears the hallmark of Drucker's influence all over them. He was a scientist in a way that he loved to spend time researching in workplace laboratories: the classrooms where he taught, the boardrooms where he counseled, and the factories where he observed. Right away, he realized the important role of the blue-collar employer to the efficiency of the corporations, and he found the best ways for top-level executives to communicate with their employees for effective production. He understood the language and concerns of those on the assembly lines, as well as the process and concerns of the executives in their towers. Drucker's ultimate skill, however, was his ability to convey best practices for running and managing business in a way that was intelligible to anyone and everyone.

To read Drucker's books is to experience a smart delivery in which no words were wasted. His rules for business flow like modern poetry. Many Drucker quotes can be found displayed in offices around the world. He possessed a philosophical as much as a business mind. If the shortest distance between two points is a straight line, then Drucker's published works are the straightest line to good business practices that there is. A daily calendar with Drucker quotations offers up with each new day a sampling of his inspiring insights.

He loved to educate and speculate about the ways to run a healthy company. Drucker wrote and published more than three dozen books and hundreds of columns for *The Wall Street Journal, The Harvard Business Review, The Atlantic Monthly, The Economist* and more. He also made eight series of educational films and several audio recordings. When you read, hear, or watch Peter Drucker expound on various subjects regarding the world of business and running a company, it is nearly impossible to come away without having gained some valuable information that can easily be put into practice.

As an invited observer to the GM Headquarters, he was able to take note of board meetings and the decision-making processes of this most powerful and productive corporation. He was allowed to walk the shop floor and interview employees. In those days, such things were never even considered, let alone allowed. That someone actually got this privilege is surprising in itself, but the book that materialized from those two years, *Concept of the Corporation*, changed the way America and its corporations thought about running a business. Drucker was unflinching in his views. His book met with success and surely inspired thousands of young business people – even if his actual sponsors at GM were unhappy with the stance his book professed. Alfred Sloan, the legendary Chairman of GM, was reputed to have been so upset with this book that no one was allowed to mention either Drucker or his books in his presence. However, it's this direct honesty and efficiency that made Drucker so valuable toward giving a shot in the arm to modern American efficiency that had loped along from the industrial revolution a century earlier, and that set the stage for the era of the computer a century later.

Drucker was able to connect with business students (in colleges or in libraries) through his poetically lean expression. He never wasted words. He put into practice the common dictum: *When in doubt, leave it out.* He didn't have much use for adjectives in his writing. Decorative phrases wasted time; not just his time, but the reader's as well, and he would never be party to that. He also spoke a plain style of English. Perhaps it was a result of English not being his original language. He was the sort of writer who you could safely read without the need of a dictionary at your side. His enduring tendency as an innovator was to break everything into simple lists. Nearly all Drucker's books have lists that work themselves into play. In fact, one of his most famous books is based on a list: *Five Most Important Questions That You Will*

Ever Ask Yourself About Your Organization. Drucker has lists explaining how to hire an executive board, a list for how human resources managers should hire employees, a list for innovating and eliminating departments, and even a list to provide managers with the ability to properly reassess how well they and their underlings are performing their assigned tasks. It is amazing to see how all manner of complex corporations could be reduced to a list, as if those complexities were collections of paper routes. By the mid-1960s, he gathered core concepts of capitalism when he prepared his notes and essays for what would become his seminal work, 1967s *The Effective Executive*, which is among the most important books in American management history for business leaders. He then spent the remainder of the century refining it and preparing his principles to be adapted for the computer age and beyond.

In *The Effective Executive*, Drucker breaks down the best practices for leading with another one of his patented lists of five best practices: Managing time, choosing what you should contribute to the organization, knowing where and how to mobilize strength to the fullest effect, setting the right priorities, and weaving them together into one cohesive unit. Where other motivational leaders in literature like Coach John Wooden of UCLA were putting their platforms together, they relied on much larger all-encompassing sets of practices, such as the Wooden Pyramid of Success, but those practices were broader than even Drucker's. Drucker's practices were also put together for the end purpose of helping the leaders help their companies to improve their bottom lines.

Even Alfred Sloan, the legendary chairman of GM, who had originally given Drucker his big break in the business world (by providing him free access at General Motors for two years), took offense at the critical observations made about the inner workings and intra-communications within GM. For decades, Sloan would simply make believe that the book and Drucker didn't even exist. Meanwhile, Drucker, as journalist, risked his future access to America's largest automobile company in standing by that critical picture that revealed his most telling trademark, his credibility. This mixture of knowledge, communications skills and journalistic integrity transformed Drucker into a reluctant guru for many and, as a result, better prepared MBA students for the fast approaching century.

Of all of Drucker's lessons and practices, probably his most important one is self-awareness, that is, holding oneself accountable for the success/failure of an organization. After all, if you are the person making the decisions, it is only natural that one turn the analysis on one's own self. Common questions like: "would you enter this field if you were 23 years old," followed immediately by a "Why" or a "Why not?" "What are your strengths and weaknesses?" "Who are your customers?" "What departments are no longer necessary?" "How do you listen?" "What areas are you the best at?" These are all necessary questions that need to be considered to be truly self-accountable. Drucker's gift was the ability to ask these questions not only to the faces of business titans, but also to college students, or to record it on audiocassette, as well as to write prolifically in a clear and concise business language.

It would be impossible to fit all of Peter Drucker's influences and writings into one book. After all, Drucker wrote nearly 40 books on his own, and he published hundreds of essays, and hundreds of thousands of words. He was one of the most prolific writers of the 20th century, and in the world of business writing, he undoubtedly led the pack. This book, by Dr. Luther Guynes, who was one of Drucker's first students carefully explains many of Drucker's primary ideas and when you have finished reading this book, you will be well versed in the writings and practices of this world-class genius. As a result, you will have a much greater awareness of what is needed to be your best business leader.

TABLE OF CONTENTS

	Acknowledgements	v
	Dr. Luther Guynes Bio	vii
	Introduction by Dr. Mike Miller, Ph.D., M.Ed., M.S.	xi
Chapter I.	Self Awareness	1
Chapter II.	Human Relations and People	15
Chapter III.	Communicating Effectively	31
Chapter IV.	Self-Assessment	49
Chapter V.	Nonprofits–Mission To Performance	63
Chapter VI.	Leadership	81
Chapter VII.	Success Through Strength	97
Chapter VIII.	Innovation	109
Chapter IX.	Decisionmaking	121
Chapter X.	Into The Future	131
	Chapter Summaries	141
	Appendix I - Guynes Family Tree	147

> **Drucker's Wisdom**
>
> Knowledge workers need to ask questions.
> What should my contribution be?

CHAPTER I

SELF AWARENESS

"Success in the knowledge economy comes to those who know themselves–their strengths, their values, and how they best perform."
–**Peter F. Drucker**, *Managing Oneself*

One of Drucker's key concepts for successful management is the belief that with self-control and self-management, one can rise to the top of their chosen profession. It's up to you to carve out your place, to know when to change course and to keep yourself engaged and productive during a work span that could last up to sixty years. Drucker says that the key to succeeding at the highest level is by understanding and relying on your strengths, knowing how you perform to accomplish your desired results and identifying your personal values. In his book, *Managing Oneself*, Drucker outlines seven steps necessary to elevate your performance to the highest possible levels. Each successful step, however, requires an understanding of one's strengths, method and values.

It is not only possible to develop ourselves from a competent level to an elite level by mastering your understanding of these three areas, it is practically impossible to reach the upper echelons if you do not master these three steps: an honest evaluation, feedback analysis, and a constant refreshing of your priority list. Drucker suggests a new manager or executive should limit his scope to no more than two years because goals change constantly and, typically, by the time you complete your first goal, the priorities of the organization or your department will have changed, thus necessitating an updated priorities list.

What Are Your Strengths?

A person can perform only from strengths. One cannot build performance on weaknesses, let alone on something one cannot do at all. Most people are not familiar with their strengths. Some people are, but most people have no idea, and as a result they are constantly facing an uphill climb that peaks at mediocrity. People want to take pride in a performance they know is well done. They want to make contributions to their organization. After all, work takes up well over a third of all one's waking hours. But it is impossible to work from your strengths if you don't know what they are.

Only when you work from your strengths can you achieve true excellence. In order to learn your strengths, you need to be honest with yourself, and persevere in your self-evaluation. Drucker stated that it takes more energy to go from incompetence to mediocrity than it does to go from being first rate to being exceptional. Therefore, to maximize your capability within a company or ability to run your own business, you and your employees must work from your strengths. However, in order to work from your strengths, you first have to know how to verify or even discover what your strengths are. Without taking this first step, you may detour yourself from your optimum peak performance by years.

In order to discover your strengths, Drucker suggests using an approach called "Feedback Analysis." Feedback Analysis is a simple but vital step to discovering both your strengths and weaknesses as an executive or manager. One begins at the dawn of a new project. Whenever you make an important decision or executive action, write it down along with your anticipated results. After a year, compare your actual results with your expectations. After two to three years, you will know where your actual strengths lie.

Before engaging in a business venture, write out your projections for where you expect to be one year in the future. Whether or not the venture is still in business after a year's time, pull out that forecast and take an honest look, for this is your ledger for what needed to be done and what has been accomplished. Update your forecast after each review. Within two to three years, you should have a very clear idea of what your strengths are. You will also have a clear idea of where you lack competence. Drucker insists that it is far easier to propel a skill set from good to great than it is to make an incompetent performer mediocre. Using a feedback analysis approach will ensure you are certain about where your strengths lie as a performer, while also providing insight into your blind spots that may need the help of teammates to shore up. The accurate knowledge of one's strengths and weaknesses as a performer is vital for achieving maximum success.

Once you know where your strengths as an executive or as a company lie, Drucker stressed that you should extend the majority of your energy toward those things that you achieve at the highest levels, so that you can become an exceptional expert in your field. You should maximize the amount of time spent improving on your strengths, and finding what things are inhibiting your strengths. Rather than wasting time and energy turning incompetent performers into competent performers, one should expend all energy toward taking competent performers and turning them into star performers.

How Do I Perform?

Once you know what your strengths are, you have to be able to answer the question **"How do I perform?"** By this, Drucker is telling you to understand your method of learning. There are any number of ways to learn (*e.g.,* reading, writing, listening, talking, note taking...) and no one or two ways are an all-mighty correct way, but for the sake of running an efficient business, there are correct and incorrect combinations of team members that can determine whether or not a company thrives, stagnates, or fails. A perfect combination of performance styles does not guarantee success; however, a juxtaposition of incompatible styles will almost certainly lead to failure, and a waste of time and resources.

Based on your learning style and approach to success, the goal is to place yourself in the best situation for your optimum success. We become our best only when we are aware of how we work best. A good starting point is to determine whether you are a listener or a reader. President FDR was a listener, President JFK, a reader. Then you have to consider, **"How do you learn?"** Some people learn best by taking extensive notes, while others learn best by reading or saying a lesson aloud. You need to become aware of your learning style.

Another important element to consider is **what kind of a work environment** is optimum for your success? Do you work best alone or in an office/team scenario? Are you best suited as a decision maker, an advisor, or a soldier? Drucker's main lesson in this area emphasizes self-control that does not seek to change yourself but, instead, tries to improve the way you perform and tries to avoid work you are destined to perform poorly due to your ingrained methodology.

If you work best as a loner, don't accept a position with a company that uses an open office style. If you do not perform at your best with PowerPoint presentations, don't take a position with a company that requires weekly presentations. Sometimes the best decisions are totally obvious, but by convincing oneself that one can completely alter their style of performing or their coworker's style is misleading and typically destined to fail.

By way of example, a sales manager hires a top sales professional from a rival company. The manager is a person whose learning methods are listening and talking. If the new sales star comes from a company where the sales manager used a reading and writing approach toward conducting team meetings, this will lead to a conflict of method approaches that is doomed to failure. The manager will expect communication by way of oral presentation, while the new sales star will show up with a great spreadsheet, but precious little to say. The new sales person will become frustrated that their spreadsheet is unread, and the manager keeps asking questions already clearly answered on the spreadsheet. The manager meanwhile will become frustrated by the new salesperson and what he perceives as a lazy, obstinate attitude toward the manager and other teammates. Both the sales manager and the sales professional may be capable of performing at a high level, and while they may both feel as if they were already performing at a high level, their conflicting styles of how to achieve success will ultimately prevent this shared goal from being accomplished.

What Are Your Values?

The third element of self-control is to know **"What are your values?"** Say you are taking over as a sales manager for a city news weekly. If your value is to focus on growing the Internet version of the magazine, but the publisher's value is to increase the readership of the print edition, there will be a conflict of values. If your values conflict with the values of the organization you are hired to improve, you will over time become frustrated and you will have subpar results. **In order to perform at your peak level, your values should match.**

Drucker uses his own personal story as an example of how he followed his theory to find a greater level of self-control and a higher peak performance on a personal level. During the 1930s, Drucker was a successful investment banker in London; however, he valued people, not "being the richest person in the cemetery." So, he quit his job, despite being in the depths of the Great

Depression, at a time when finding employment was far from certain. He chose to go with his values, because without the element of personal values, the employee is only left with a paycheck for motivation, which eventually leads to poor performance. Another example would be a corporate attorney who leaves to start a small-town practice. Values can change over time. For example, upon graduation with a large student loan debt, values can be placed on hold to level your finances. Even so, to reach one's peak performance level, an individual and an organization should be in agreement when it comes to values. Drucker states that "Values are and should be the ultimate test."

Know Where You Belong

Drucker also stressed that in order to peak perform, you need to **"know where you belong."** According to his lessons, where you belong is where strengths, your style of performance, and your values intersect. Most gifted people do not know where they belong until they have passed their twenties but he says that, by that time, they should be able to answer the three key questions:

"What are my strengths, how do I perform, and what are my values, and then they can and should decide where they belong."

This also means they know where they do not belong. By this point, they should know whether they don't belong in an office setting, or if they do not belong in a company that relies on spread sheets. The person who knows whether they are not a decision maker, should know not to accept that kind of position. If you pursue a position with an organization where you clearly don't belong, you are in all actuality pursuing headaches, frustration and ultimately professional failure to contribute meaningful growth.

By the same token, to know the answers to these questions provides the knowledge to not only select which organization is best for you and where you can contribute best, you can also inform the organization how you can best handle the job, and what will be necessary so that you can be entrusted to maximize your contribution to the highest level. You can accurately provide your organization with what they can expect from you in what kind of a time frame, because you know who you are and how you fit in with the organization. Knowing where you belong can turn an otherwise ordinary performer into an outstanding performer.

What Should You Contribute?

Once you assume the position within the organization, you need to figure out what you should contribute to the company. Drucker interprets the contribution as how one can improve the company's bottom line. Knowledge workers need to ask themselves, "What should my contribution be?" The answer, Drucker said, would be found by asking the following **three questions**: "What does the situation require? Given my strengths, my way of performing and my values, how can I make the greatest contribution to what needs to be done? What results have to be achieved to make a difference?" He points out that, typically, any planning that extends beyond 18 months to two years rarely comes to fruition; one should focus on what can be accomplished within the first year and a half.

These contributions should be hard to reach, yet reachable. If it's too easy, then it's not worth it, and if it's impossible to reach, then one is setting themselves up for failure. It's important to find the right balance between the two. The contribution should also be meaningful. There has to be a purpose or a benefit to one's contribution for it to have any positive effect. Finally, the contribution has to be visible and preferably measurable. After eighteen months, one should be able to show their results, which will directly correlate with the contributions one brings to the organization, and what needs to be done to escalate the contributions. *"What gets measured, gets managed"* **–Peter Drucker.**

Take Responsibility For Your Relationships

Once you are in your position, you need to take responsibility for your relationships. Since most people work with others, they need to be effective with other people. You must accept the fact that most people are individuals, with their own strengths, methods, and values, so to be effective, one must take responsibility to meet your co-worker and find out who they are. Bosses are entitled to work the way they work to do their job most effectively, and it is up to the employees to understand how the boss works and adapt themselves to what makes their bosses most effective. How your coworkers perform is of less value than their strengths and values.

One must also take responsibility for communication. Personality conflicts arise from workers not understanding each other's contributions. With the specialization of knowledge workers in executive positions, people are often working within their task bubble. It is the responsibility of each associate to understand what each worker is contributing. This can be done easiest by asking. Drucker suggests inter-sectional get-togethers where workers can familiarize themselves with the tasks and contributions of workers in other departments. This way each department can be on the same page, while being focused on the different tasks. By understanding how each piece of the organization fits, a company can perform work together to a peak level.

This takes some work, and, indeed, for some people introducing yourself to strangers can be daunting, but to be the best at your position and to optimize your benefit to your company, you need to face and overcome this obstacle. And, it will also make your job a lot easier. This doesn't mean that you have to introduce yourself to the parking lot attendants and ask them about parking methodology, but, at the very least, you should familiarize yourself with all your regular and even occasional coworkers with whom you intersect on completing tasks. Know what everyone else does to make the organization run efficiently. Have a paintbrush understanding of what these people may need from you to make your day and theirs pass with less stress.

The Second Half of Your Life

Drucker put an emphasis on taking control of the second half of your life. Unlike the laborers of the first half of the twentieth century, knowledge workers are not finished working after four decades on the job. They are typically at the peak of their professional performance, and they are certainly experts at their job, but they will get bored because they are no longer able to challenge themselves. At the same time, they are often facing an additional 25 years at the same position of the same company. That is hardly a satisfying work life. They are at their peaks professionally, but, by mid-forties, they often feel that they have nowhere to grow as an executive. Drucker suggests that a solution to the mid-life career crisis is to start a second career.

Drucker suggests three primary directions one can take to prepare for an alternate career during the second half of your professional life: 1) start a career in a different type of organization, 2) take a side job in something that appeals specifically to your values for less or no money, or 3) start an activity or an organization or nonprofit in an area that interests you. He suggests that initiating steps toward an alternate career path must begin prior to one's 40s. Those who enter the second half career path after age 40 have a far lesser likelihood to succeed, so, for career satisfaction that extends beyond reaching the excellence in your area of knowledge and sustains one for their entire life, pursuing the following steps is essential:

A man whom we'll call "Jake", for example, has spent 25 years building a highly lucrative and successful career as a corporate attorney for a large franchise. Jake specializes in branding, and at this point in his career, he is not only considered an expert, but one of the top achievers in his area of knowledge, that being franchise-level fashion branding protection. However, after 25 years, Jake no longer feels a passion for his career. This is because, after so many years of being at the top of his industry, he has stopped learning, and is therefore at a crisis when it comes to finding ways to contribute in a meaningful way, while staying true to his value system. Now, Jake is approaching 50, with an additional 20 years of time remaining in his work life and is facing a career crossroads. Can Jake maintain his level of enthusiasm at his current position for the rest of his work life? What options does Jake have if he separates himself from his current organization?

Perhaps Jake could have set aside ten hours a week to provide general legal services at a nonprofit. If he began this side charity work in his mid-30s, he would have already established an unofficial second practice, albeit at a much smaller level. Perhaps, he can downshift to a small-town private practice, or he can begin accepting cases as a public defender.

Here is a scenario where Jake can create a second half career by way of creating a non-profit. Suppose Jake were an avid bicyclist as a way of relaxation and as an alternate way of commuting that exists within his value system (which happens to include leaving a reduced carbon footprint), Jake could establish a non-profit centered around cycling and encouraging cycling as a means of mobility. If Jake begins his involvement when he is 25 years old, he will have over two decades of experience and relationship building in the areas of alternative mobility, cycling and green commuting. Now at 50, Jake has an opportunity to create a second career because he has inadvertently become an expert in his secondary field, and because his value system is fulfilled to a level where it negates his financial concerns.

Another possibility could be for Jake to take a side job–something that might break things up in his daily routine. Perhaps he accepts a 10 hour-a-week assignment as a tutor. Maybe, it's expanding a hobby like photography into a second job or, as Drucker would interpret it, a "side hustle." As your bank account grows and your interest in your primary job recedes, a secondary parallel job can eventually take over as a primary career.

Drucker asserts however, that any plan for a second half career has to be taken before reaching your 40s, otherwise, the likelihood of following through with the later life plans will inevitably fall short. Part of this is that a knowledge worker who has reached the peak of their position will be less inclined to start from scratch. In all of the successful examples for Jake, he had taken several years at his secondary job before he was qualified to make a responsible shift. A second half career is not the same thing as a parallel move from one company and position to another similar type of company and position. A second half career is more drastic, and if done correctly, both more lasting and more personally satisfying. You will also have the greatest chance at reaching a level of excellence with a second career that is not thought up on the fly. This is why it is as vital to take control of your later years as it is to live in the moment professionally.

Summary

Drucker's theory of self-management, the keys to properly controlling and managing one's self to maximize peak professional performance, requires following the previously stated seven steps to self-management. Know what your strengths are. Know how you perform. Know what your values are. Know where you belong. Understand what you should contribute. Take responsibility for your relationships. Prepare for the second half of professional life. Following these steps, you should not only be able to maximize one career, but multiple careers. A happier professional life is a healthier life. Drucker's breakthroughs in self-management have made professional lives more fulfilling for millions of people.

> **Drucker's Wisdom**
>
> The four requirements of human relations: communication, teamwork, self-development and development of others.

CHAPTER II

HUMAN RELATIONS AND PEOPLE

In his 1974 book, *Management: Tasks, Responsibilities, Practices*, Drucker emphasizes that of all the many decisions made by an organization, people decisions are the most important to get correct. Since each position is reliant on other departments running smoothly, an unsuccessful hire at, say, a regional assistant manager level can produce an immediate negative affect on an organization's bottom line. Drucker recognized what worked in the past and, as always, streamlined the process to make it adaptable to any organization.

He based his methodology on the successes of US General George C. Marshall's selection of World War II officers and by corporate and plant management selections made by GM CEO Alfred Sloan. Drucker identifies **five decision steps** that successful managers take regarding people decisions and five corresponding and equally necessary ground rules to make the correct choices. By closely following these steps, an executive or manager in charge of hiring increases their chances for success.

First, think carefully through the work assignment. Job descriptions are concrete, while job assignments typically remain fluid. Different assignments require different types of people. In order for you to successfully select the person to fill an important leadership position, you need to understand what kind of strengths are most important for a team leader to achieve success. If you don't know what success is supposed to be, you won't be able to achieve it.

Second, look at several qualified people. If you're buying an car or a house, you don't simply buy the first one that meets your basic expectations. You would look for what other options might be available. If the first candidate matches your job description, that doesn't mean your search should end with that candidate. Seek out at least four or five candidates. That way, you may discover additional strengths that you may not have thought about previously and which may benefit the company. You have one shot at hiring a perfect candidate to run each knowledge position in your organization. Mistakes can cost the bottom line millions. Put the time into checking at least a handful of qualified candidates before making a final decision.

Third, you should always study the performance record of the candidates. During Drucker's time, this would have been done by vetting a candidate's resume. These days, those in charge of making people decisions can rely on social networks and social media. *LinkedIn* is a constantly morphing source of candidate information. It doesn't just list resumes, it also lists skills and endorsements for those skills by people with whom someone has presumably had business relationships. A resume with many positions at different companies over a short period may raise a red flag that this candidate may be non-committal. It could also mean, however, that they have worked at several startups or pharmaceutical companies where turnover is a common part of the professional life. By studying the records of individual candidates, you're holding a magnifying glass over a chart of a candidate's strengths and weaknesses.

Fourth, a person in charge of making people decisions should reach out to people who have worked with them before. A candidate's previous coworkers or supervisors can provide all sorts of insight into the strengths of a candidate and it also provides firsthand information about how a person works in the field. This additional insight is invaluable as it can determine how great their strengths are, as well as how they compensate for their weaknesses. If hiring from within the company, a decision maker will have a better idea of how a new manager might affect morale and production at the ground level. Many executives and human resource managers don't spend a lot of time inside factories or in sales meetings or in some warehouse stocking shelves. It is extremely beneficial to take advantage of the personnel experts who are already on your payroll. Company morale will also benefit, because everyone feels that they are a part of the decision, and subordinates will support a new manager and work together for success accordingly.

Lastly, always make sure that the new manager knows exactly how success is to be measured. If a new manager doesn't know what this is, they have no way of succeeding. If the goal of a farmer's market is to acquire more new vendors, let the new manager know that their success or failure will be based on this measure. If the expectation is to raise the average revenue per booth, then that needs to be made clear. After 90 days, have the new manager submit a forecast report in writing. After nine months to a year, you will know if you made the correct choice and why. If you made the incorrect choice, adjust and either fire the failing manager or offer them their old position back. Ultimately, the buck stops with you, so you must be willing to accept the responsibility and shoulder the blame if the hiring doesn't work out and, then, move on. However, if you follow these five steps, your likelihood of success will increase exponentially.

Incorporate feedback into all your decisions. It's good practice, and it also holds everyone accountable for what is expected of them while they are in the position. Drucker was adamant about allowing an "exit plan" for employees who have a proven track record at their natural position but are being given an opportunity to stretch their professional wings. Not every promotion will pan out, but the company will still benefit by maintaining all their experts, regardless of position. Let a candidate know that if a promotion doesn't work out, they will still have great value at their previous position. Some failed candidates may take offense at a demotion, but many great employees will be glad to return to the position they're good at. If you see a position where two or more managers in a row have failed, kill the position, and wait until the company has resettled. Only then should you refill the position.

In summary, Drucker essentially breaks down people decision making into **five steps**: 1) think through the assignment carefully; 2) look at several qualified candidates; 3) consider the candidates' strengths; 4) discuss the candidates with colleagues and coworkers; and 5) make sure that the appointee is aware of what is expected of them for success.

Along with these steps, Drucker recommended these rules: accept responsibility for any people decision, including failures; accept that failed performers need to be removed; soldiers deserve competent commanders; it is the manager's decision to make the correct people decisions every time and for every position; and all hired staff should be entering with an awareness of their expectations and that proper tools are made available for them to succeed.

Up until the late 20th century, there were two contrasting philosophies toward work and workers. These theories were written about in Douglas McGregor's book, *The Human Side of Enterprise* (1960). Theory X, the traditional approach to workers and working, presumes that workers are not motivated and need to be commanded and controlled. Theory Y contends that workers can be self-motivated and self-controlled. Drucker, of course, recognized that neither Theory X nor Theory Y was fully correct.

Great fear coerces, while loose ends are more likely to cause resentment. Lesser fears weaken motivation due to a lessening of authority. Even so, if an organization simply hands over the carrot, production will also suffer, for it is specifically the rising level of material expectations that makes the carrot of material reward less and less effective as a motivating force and as a managerial tool. By themselves, combinations of fear and money are not enough to maintain optimal production in the long run. To achieve a more perfect production, economy, fear, production, and satisfaction need to be balanced. Human resources can connect these competing but, ultimately, complementary parts. When human resources works effectively, workers are more productive and more satisfied and the organization benefits as a result.

In his book, *The Effective Executive*, Drucker definitively states that "knowledge workers in an organization do not have good human relations because they have a 'talent for people.' They have good human relations because they focus on contribution in their own work and in their relationship with others. As a result, their relationships are productive–and this is the only valid definition of 'good human relations.'"

In other words, a human relations department should not be filled with so called "people persons," they should be filled with team players who specialize in placing the best people into the best positions for them to succeed at their highest levels for the benefit of the company's goals–long-term and short-term. They need to be able to identify talents of people as well as to identify a company's needs. Only by identifying and properly synchronizing needs, strengths and benefits for the organization as a whole is a good human relations department truly effective. It's amazing how Drucker's lessons have remained ironclad in the 50+ years since the book's original publication. His four basic requirements of human relations remain as true today as they did in 1967.

FOUR BASIC REQUIREMENTS OF HUMAN RELATIONS
1. Communications
2. Teamwork
3. Self-development
4. Development of others

COMMUNICATIONS

> *"Communications are practically impossible if they're based on a downward relationship."*

The harder that a superior tries to be heard, the harder the subordinate will unhear what is being told to them, and instead they will hear what they expect to hear. In other words, they will effectively drown out their manager. In popular culture terms, think of the adult characters in Charles Schulz's *Charlie Brown* cartoons. The adults are the superiors to the children, yet whenever the children (representing the viewers) are spoken to by adults, all they hear are unintelligible tones. Meanwhile, the children, who in this case would be the subordinates, are heard clearly when they speak to the adults or the viewers.

Instead of speaking down to employees, hold those employees accountable for their role within the company and their expected contribution. Find out what their strengths are and in which areas they are expert. Together, discuss how they can best use their strengths and expertise for the optimum benefit to the organization. Once goals are agreed upon, a superior has the right to expect the subordinate to be accountable for what has been agreed to as their contribution. In this post-Drucker world, these would be spreadsheets.

Studies have shown that typically what the subordinate sees as the appropriate contribution rarely matches what the superior sees as the appropriate contribution. This is because the two come from two different perspectives. For example, a sales V.P. in a centralized corporate office in Chicago may not be familiar with the street level reality for a door-to-door salesmen in Bettendorf, Iowa. When the subordinate is treated as an expert in their area, in this case selling in a region of Iowa, the superior can then determine how well the subordinate is achieving, and only then can they effectively determine how much to raise or lower their monthly and quarterly goals in order to maximize the office's production target.

At the end of the day, what is not important is who is correct when it comes to determine the workloads and the expectations of the relationship. What does matter is that there is an effective road of communication. As long as this communication is in place, contributions can be monitored and stimulated.

Teamwork

The reality of knowledgeable organizations is that teams of people with diverse knowledge and skills combine to effectively get the work done. These people coordinate their work together, depending on the task at hand and the logic of the situation. Often, there are several teams consisting of multiple employees, with little knowledge of what other similarly staffed teams are working towards. In any case, an effective team, much like any effective organization, must have similar long-term goals for the overall organization. Each has to keep the others informed of what is happening on their ends because, without some sort of coordination between the separate departments, their efforts are more likely to do damage than to help.

For example, an advertising executive for a magazine sells ads to a client organization. An ad copy staffer may then draw the initial layout of the advertisement while providing the key text – the words to sell the product. The ad is co-created by copywriters, proofreaders, photographers, illustrators, graphic artists, pre-press operators, a design director and a publisher, before the advertisement is printed in the magazine. If there are issues with the payment of the advertisement, the accounting staff notifies the initial salesperson to remedy the situation, otherwise a payments receivable department may be involved. This is the team for a single ad, and there are other people involved as well from within the company and working on a freelance basis. They all work together at their various skills and areas of expertise, both together and separately, dozens of times to complete the ads for the magazine. Meanwhile, a separate, but equally important editorial team is putting together the editorial content. Another completely different team handles distribution. These various factions and teams may not be familiar with each area of expertise, but if one member of the team does not carry his or her weight, it can affect the final results for the entire operation. It's essential that, regardless of whatever role one works in the company, whether it be executive, manager or employee, everyone has the same goal for the organization to maximize its overall efficiency.

Drucker teaches that individual self-development in large measure depends on their focus on contributions. An effective employee should ask themselves how they can most contribute their strengths for the greatest benefit for their company. That way they can know what areas need further development. In a post-Drucker world, an example of this would be updating one's knowledge in the latest technology, software and applications. Once their strengths are acknowledged and their strategy is in place, an employee can work to improve from *very good* to *exceptional*, and with the increased benefits to the company, the employee will also receive a greater sense of self-worth.

Development of Others

Drucker points out that "the executive who focuses on contribution also stimulates others to develop themselves, whether they are subordinates, colleagues or superiors." The standards are not based on any sort of preference, but rather by what needs to be done. There must be demands for the highest possible standards. Their demands must inspire high aspiration and ambitious goals. The classic example of this is the manager or executive who is early to work, constantly updating his or her skill set, and who is prepared to excel at their work and to inspire and propel their subordinates to strive for equally ambitious individual and team goals. People improve themselves by placing higher demands on themselves. A good manager can be the cue to the rest of the team to push themselves harder than they believe possible. As Drucker says, *"If they demand little of themselves, they will remain stunted. If they demand a good deal of themselves, they will grow to giant stature–without any more effort than the underachievers."*

Drucker had the foresight to be the first business intellectual to emphasize the importance of maintaining allegiance and continued work relationships with experts as they age out into retirement. He was the first to suggest that institutions of business adapt or create programs similar to the emeritus positions used in universities. These positions are commonplace in today's business world, but in 1974 when he wrote about it in his book *Management*, thoughts like these were revolutionary.

> "Enterprises must attract, hold, and make productive people who have reached official retirement age, have become independent outside contractors, or are not available as full time permanent employees, for example, highly skilled and educated older people, instead of being retired, might be offered a choice of continuing relationships that convert them into long-term "inside-outsiders," preserving their skill and knowledge for the enterprise and yet giving them the flexibility and freedom they expect and can afford." –*Management* (1974)

Good human relations in a business atmosphere is a continuous balancing act between personal satisfaction of the worker and maximum production for the organization. Drucker said it best when he wrote that "personal satisfaction of the worker without productive work is failure, but so is productive work that destroys the worker's achievement. Neither is, in effect, tenable for long."

THE FIVE DIMENSIONS OF WORKING

Drucker writes that there are **five dimensions to working**, which encompass both the personal and the communal. Each dimension is equally important, and one cannot work properly if they are not all accounted for. The five dimensions are: physiological; psychological; social; economic; and power. If one dimension is ignored, the others will inevitably suffer.

Physiological

A human excels in relating perception to action and works best if the entire person–muscles, senses and mind, is engaged by the work. If a person is outgoing, a position requiring solitary confinement may not be a good fit. To stay motivated, a puzzle solver may be better off in a position requiring that sort of intellect, while an athlete may be more suited for a position requiring physical labor.

While work is work, and most efficient when properly matched with the worker, working is best organized with a considerable degree of diversity. An employee is not a piece of machinery, but a human. A person can't stamp a plate over and over again 40 hours-a-week, 250 days-a-year, while maintaining any interest in their performance, let alone pride in their position within the company. Diversity of task keeps workers engaged at a higher level, and allows them to develop greater pride in their position within the corporate team.

Psychological

Work is an extension of personality. It is one of the ways in which a person defines themselves and measures their worth and humanity. People want to feel proud of what they do for a living. When two people are introduced for the first time, more often than not, one of the first few pieces of information to be exchanged is what each person does for a living. So it is vital that employees take *ownership* of their role within their organization and the only way for that to occur is if an employee takes *pride* in their role within their organization.

Drucker dates our Western work ethic to 6th century Benedictine Monks of Nursia who believed that all work is service and contribution and equally deserving of respect. It was believed that the harder one worked, the closer one came to God.

A further comparison came to Drucker when he compared our work ethic to the expectations of retired workers in Confucian society. The elders were expected to reflect on the lessons learned over a lifetime of service. These elders' tasks were considered of even greater value than all their social contribution. In fact, this tradition remains today with emeritus members of many organizations as experts with decades of contributions and lessons to be passed down to future generations.

Drucker points out that many improvements to the psychological dimension are due to advances in nutrition, which greatly increases the physical energy available for work. Quality nutrition also reduces internal obstacles like depression, which can occur, among other things, when one is nutritionally deprived. In modern times, the psychological dimension is often served by things we now take for granted on the job, things like scheduled break times or lunch hours. An effective manager can use a time clock as a motivational tool by saying simply: "One more hour and we go home. Let's finish strong!" Drucker asserts that ultimately the task is still to make work serve the psychological needs of humanity.

Social

Work is a social and community bond. It largely determines status, and the person's position in society and their role within the community. People put it on their business cards directly under their name. In some instances, such as with a coach, a doctor or a military officer, a person's job title actually replaces his or her birth name. Drucker paraphrases Aristotle when he says that we need work to satisfy our need for community. In the 21st century, terms like "work-spouse" and "work-family" further cement this notion. What was true 2,500 years ago in Greece remains true today. Work is the place where we spend most of our time outside our home, and it's the place where we work toward common short term and long term goals.

Although work and a person's position within an organization may define his or her community status, it is not unusual to find someone who ranks low socially in a work group but who is a big shot somewhere else. In most cases, however, people are reliant on work to provide much of their companionship, group identification and social bond. Work is, for most people, the one bond outside of their family or household. An effective company understands this notion, and they encourage the bond among employees, but it should always keep an eye on the long-term benefits for the organization.

Drucker describes the workplace as a second community, a primary social club, a sole means of escaping loneliness, whether someone is single, divorced, widowed or with a spouse who also works, and/or children who have moved out.

According to Drucker every company which polled its retired employees were nearly unanimous in their reactions. What the retired workers missed most were their work peers, old colleagues and friends. They would even recall nice feelings for people they despised when they worked together. The human relationship in the workplace has an objective and an outside focus besides the work itself.

Economic

We all need money. While the social element is an important part of people's human experience, people still have rent and bills to pay. Wages needs to be predictable, continuous, and adequate. If employees are unable to pay for their shelter, essentials and food, this will admit outside forces to overwhelm their production. Human Relations in the modern workplace tends to absorb the responsibilities for a worker's outside necessities.

Examples of this include traditional benefits such as health and retirement plans.

Workers need to take ownership of their departments, and there's a correlation between income and ownership. The most current example is in the world of professional sports where the word "respect" is a veiled term meaning money. However, just like in the world of business, if a player receives a maximum contract and doesn't play up to the contractual expectations in return for the financial security, the team will be crippled for the long term. Higher salaries work best and are generally only effective in highly profitable businesses. A commission structure is one solution, when applicable, where economic rewards can be expected to continue to rise in direct correlation to a worker's increased production.

Power

Many of the earliest beliefs toward management and employees assumed that employees didn't actually want to work, and therefore needed a stern rod in order to get the desired production. This was known as the carrot and stick approach. Time clocks are a remnant of the former approach. The organization member's will is subordinated to an alien will. Power and economics are inextricably tied together in the modern organization. As long as economics is a defining factor in production, there needs to be people in place to make final determinations.

> *"Apportioning the economic rewards of the members of the institution demands a central organ of authority with power of decision."*
> –**Peter F. Drucker**

Power and economics create two major countervailing power relationships – management and labor. More than this, various groups within any workforce can develop intense competition with each other. As Drucker pointed out certain inevitabilities will always occur. Redistribution of power and funds is something that no modern organization, especially a business enterprise, can escape. As mentioned prior, there is no dominant dimension. As the saying goes, "One cannot have a hand. The whole body comes with it." That is why all dimensions must be considered.

Drucker anticipated the current information age and predicted that new jobs would be opened in areas that we could never have imagined 50 years ago. He pointed out that every workers era or industrial revolution creates new categories and sources of information in the human resources that successful organizations take advantage of. Positions such as social network manager or intra-corporate event planner did not exist during Drucker's lifetime, and yet he completely understood the idea of positions being born out of cultural and technological change. And as we approach the middle of the 21st century, people decisions will remain the most important decisions that all organizations make.

> **Drucker's Wisdom**
>
> What is our mission? Who is our customer?
> What does the customer value?
> What are our results?

CHAPTER III

COMMUNICATING EFFECTIVELY

Four Fundamentals of Communication
1. Communication is Perception.
2. Communication is Expectation.
3. Communication makes Demands.
4. Communication and information are different and indeed largely opposite–yet interdependent.
  –Peter Drucker, *Drucker on Management*, 1973

Drucker said that, in business management, communication is the most important element. He described it as the one element that businesses and philosophers spend the most time and the most money. Yet, as he lamented, they rarely get anything correct.

"Communication is perception, expectation and demand."

One of the primary reasons for failing to communicate is that many executives don't have an instinct for properly communicating with their staff. Prior to Drucker's studies, no one really focused on the employees on the lower levels of a company, such as the minimum wage workers, members of the assembly line, road salesmen, or customer service workers. Prior to Drucker, communicating was too often believed to come from top officers down, when communication should actually come from the bottom up. This is because punch-clock workers cannot be expected to understand the language of people in executive, corporate or managerial suites. Communication only happens when the recipient understands what is being communicated to them in terms of their experience. If an executive from Maytag Washing Machines wants to improve their bottom line and increase productivity, ideas need to be transmitted in the language of assembly lines, truck drivers, road salesman and showroom sales team.

The recipient initiates the communication. The person emitting communications is only sound if someone can listen and understand. Drucker referred to a quote from Plato, "One must speak in the language of the recipient's experience. When talking to carpenters, use a carpenter's jargon." If you talk to a carpenter in a language that he or she understands, they can answer your questions. You can let them know what the team goal is and they can, in turn, let you know what they can do, what they need to get it done, and how long it will take to complete the task. At this point, the carpenter can be held accountable to complete X amount of production in Y amount of time. Write it down. At a predetermined period (2-4 weeks,) revisit the original agreement and determine how the progress is going. What is succeeding, what is failing. Why? What kinds of unforeseen benefits are resulting? Why? Who is succeeding at the new goals better than you expected? Why? The ultimate goal is to get the people at the bottom of the wage scale to buy in and take ownership of the project and the health of the organization.

Drucker succinctly explained in 1974,

> *"There is no possibility of communication unless we first know what the recipient, the true communicator, can see and why. Before we can communicate, we must know what the recipient expects to see and hear."*

Essentially, he was saying, that if you walk into a lab and you talk to scientists like they are sales executives, the recipients will tune out what you are trying to say. If the head of an automobile company needs to communicate an initiative to increase production by 20 percent to a warehouse full of assembly line workers in Michigan, that executive might to be able to communicate with MBA vocabulary but the line workers won't understand and their ability to receive the communication will be limited. Drucker explained that a CEO of General Motors recognized this and would often devote hours of executive board meetings to thoroughly determine which plant managers to hire. The CEO and Drucker both recognized and emphasized that it is important to delegate authority to managerial experts at knowledge work. Managers on site are valuable because they can relay the concerns of the workers to a higher level, namely, what needs to be done to reach the goals and when they can expect to complete the goals.

Communication always makes demands. It always appeals to motivation for someone to do something or to believe something. If it goes against a recipient's aspirations, values and motivations, it is not likely to be received or, at worst, resisted. There is no communication unless the recipient is willing to incorporate it into their own values.

Whereas communication is perception, information is logic. The value of information presupposes good communication. Indeed, all communication has to be focused on the productivity of the company, otherwise a company may weaken and fail.

Information cannot travel downward, it has to travel upward, otherwise, it won't be perceived properly. Coal miners do not understand the language of the executives of an energy company, nor should they be expected to. The coal miners, like assembly line employees, have specialized knowledge. If you try to communicate expectations in business school jargon, they will block you out because they cannot understand what you are asking them to do. This is why hiring the correct managers is so important. They can relay the information up channels, and thereby create communication streams.

Drucker looked ahead, past the end of the 20th century. He emphasized in 1999, that to produce information executives need for their work, they have to begin with **two questions**:

> *"What information do I owe to the people with whom I work and on whom I depend? In what form? And in what time frame?"*
> *"What information do I need myself? From whom? What form? And in what time frame?"*

He said an executive needs to ask themselves first to what and to whom do they owe information, because it establishes the need for good communication. By asking "To whom do I owe this information so that they can do their work?" He emphasized that all communications emphasize the common task, the common goals, and the common work.

The first effective question that you always need to ask yourself is:

"What do you want from me?" "Who are these other people?"

Only then can one ask:

"What information do I need? From whom? In what way? In what time frame?"

You are hiring experts in their field to handle tasks for you and the company so that you can devote most of your personal energy towards completing more high-level tasks. This is why you have to approach these experts as knowledge workers. You need to hear what their concerns are, what kind of work they can provide you, and how much time, budget and manpower will be necessary to complete said tasks. Only with that information and a shared understanding can you begin to communicate what you need to be done, and now you can ask the contracting candidate questions in their own language to accomplish the most with the end goal being the success of the organization.

Give the candidates the respect that their knowledge warrants, since you will need to depend on these people to gauge the success of their departments. A bad hire of an assistant manager in a plant in Peoria, IL, can cost a company millions if it clogs an assembly line or a distribution chain. It is important to be able to communicate with people in all branches of the company and to have people on all levels of the company who can relay their concerns and report upward.

As a top executive effective at communicating, you have to ask yourself what you need to do to help your staff achieve the company goals. Relationships must be built. If you don't know what items are needed, by whom, and for what reason, you will never be able to effectively communicate. After the people who will be working for you know what you need, only then can you ask what you need from your staff, which people are best equipped to provide you the information in the way that you need it and, then, you will have the correct idea of when this task can be expected to be completed.

At a 1979 symposium, Drucker first asked an audience to write down what they do or don't do and what helps them as managers; second, he suggested determining what other people who work in other departments in his company–his subordinates and peers–do that benefits or hampers the manager; third, he emphasized figuring out which areas of their performance are being done with excellence.

He suggests finding people who succeed at what they do, travelling to them if necessary, and finding out what they do. Write it down and see how you can put that into practice at your organization. This is not too different from modern motivation books, but that was 1979.

He also points out that this needs to start at the top of the food chain. The proper spirit needs to start at the President's office and not on the shop floor. Have the spirit prevalent in the president's office and, then, you can work on the people on the bottom of the pay scale earning minimum wage. If you don't start with yourself, then it isn't going to take.

Drucker was an enthusiastic endorser of adapting to modern technology but saw that without building relationships, information becomes mere data. He recognized that new technology might make communication easier and might ultimately create new streams of employment as well as additional streams of revenue. He recognized that as computer technologies would be adapted into modern business management environment, it would free up the company's most valuable asset, time–and in certain cases, an employee's travel time. E-mails, Skype accounts, spreadsheets, conference calls, group texts, intra-conference calls are all modern technological advances that allow a team to maximize their geographic reach while keeping as many people as possible in the office, where they can be more productive.

Today's notion of working from home would have been impractical during the majority of Drucker's peak innovative years, but these days it is a viable alternative that not only saves an organization's overall budget, but, as an unintended but extra benefit, helps to reduce traffic, road damage and urban pollution. However, as always, Drucker's primary focus concerned the many ways that technological advancements benefit the company's bottom line. Better communications means higher productivity. Meetings should be held for a purpose. If they are not productive, then they are a waste of time and have a negative effect on the organization's overall productivity. Enhanced technology is something that will enable managers to shift resources to increase productivity. Advanced technology allows organizations to improve other areas of infrastructure.

Drucker emphasized that the great obstacle of resistance to productivity in an organization is a negative consequence of a company's lack of spirit. He pointed out correctly that high levels of excitement have to come from the highest offices. If communication travels from bottom to top, it must be excitement and commitment that travels from top to bottom. That means that the CEO, executives and managers have to be the most enthusiastic toward achieving a team's goals; otherwise, the essential level of excitement will never reach the floor level workers.

Asked about getting production and participation at the hourly worker level (the shop floor), getting participation in the work force is key. Drucker challenged businesses and unions to search for ways to give workers control over their work environment. He pointed out that unions tend to come into a shop where management has not done the job they ought to. He said that if a clearly innovative vision doesn't start with the top executives themselves, the productivity will never take off. Due to the changing nature of business in the 21st century, unions have come to play an increasingly smaller role overall. In government organizations, unions still have a strong presence, but there are fewer career tracks that are so dangerous or poorly run that they require unions in that respect. The business world needs to always focus on innovation as the world always changes. Even so, unions still fight to protect worker wages and benefits. New unions entering an organization, however, raise a red flag and question the fitness and respect of an organization as perceived from the bottom.

Drucker pointed out that unions were not healthy for businesses because they typically benefitted an outdated work economy. They negatively affect productivity and can serve as an impediment to progress. The evolution of worker environments and how we work as a nation has essentially rendered traditional unions obsolete. In order for unions to stay relevant, Drucker said they have to become political. Drucker always said that there is a difference between productivity and orderliness. He said,

"Growth is disorderly, and if growth endangers productivity, it isn't growth at all, but cancer."

He said that the main purpose of growth is to "shift resources out of yesterday at the risk of shrinkage."

According to the former publisher and CEO of the Los Angeles Times Mark Willes, Drucker met with him in 1995 acting as an advisor. The newspaper was struggling to maintain its readership after a peak of more than 1.2 million daily subscribers and more than 1.5 million Sunday subscribers. The Times benefitted from the 1990 closing of the rival Herald Examiner, with their circulation peaking a few years later. The recession cost them newspaper subscribers, however, and they were also beginning to foresee an emerging rival to traditional print media, the internet. At the time of the meeting, Willes had just entered the publishing world after 15 years working for cereal giant, General Mills. Drucker was able to break down the media giant's crisis and, within four hours, was able to describe a strategy that the newspaper continued to use until it was sold to Tribune Corp in 1999 when Willes left the company.

The newspaper's initial concern was that they were failing to reach as many advertisers befitting their circulation. Drucker pointed out that the key to expanding the newspaper's market was to treat the newspaper like a series of magazines. Instead of sections, these "magazines" would target specific audiences. Instead of having editors as their section heads, they would assign "general managers." At the time, such thinking was revolutionary! They would think of their newspaper as a business, instead of a newspaper.

Certain changes, such as regional issues like Orange County, San Fernando Valley, and Inland Valley Voice editions were successful for nearly a decade after the meeting. Other areas of targeting included Sunday magazines with a concerted effort towards luring Spanish language readers to special editions. Each general manager would be assigned a team of sales staff with one purpose, to raise circulation and, more importantly, to bring in new advertisers and raise revenue for the section, which would ultimately nourish the entire newspaper. As a result of the overall efforts, the Los Angeles Times circulation managed to stay above a million daily subscribers well beyond the sale of the newspaper by the Chandler family until 2004, and nearly an entire decade after the publisher and CEO sat down with Drucker for four hours to discuss the newspaper.

How would those lessons apply into the 21st century? Well, by the time the Los Angeles Times circulation dropped below a million daily subscribers in 2004, there was a new possibility for revenue streams to make it up. Drucker always believed that to stay ahead of the times, a smart company will embrace change, especially communications changes, and be at the vanguard of new communications technologies. Changes have to come from the top. Newspapers were required to embrace the internet. Internet websites like *Craigslist* were devouring revenue from traditional newspapers. Smart newspapers discovered that they could reproduce their publications onto their own websites, but that along with convincing readers to seek out and ultimately pay to read the news online, the publisher also has to convince a sales staff to sell internet ads with as much commitment as they sold traditional print ads.

This must have been a monumental task, as it would require sales performers to maintain their print ad quotas while also establishing web ad quotas, and while educating advertisers as to the value of the web and convincing them to buy. This would require leaps of faith that can only come from masterful communication to sell a salesperson's belief. However, for the sales team to effectively build legitimate excitement for a new program, the greatest and most original excitement has to come from the highest of sources, the CEO and the Publisher. Build the excitement, explain new changes and why it is a great thing for the company as a whole, and then ask the staff what needs to be done to make this happen. Orders can come from the top, but the questions and the communication must come from the people who meet the goals, the sales team.

Willes described his four-hour consultation with Drucker to be something that he would refer back to for years afterward. He said that he implemented suggestions from that meeting all the way to the end of his tenure as publisher, several years later, when the newspaper was sold to Tribune Media. He never had to implement the greatest change and challenge facing post-modern media, namely, how do newspapers adapt to the open and uncontrolled internet? This is probably how Drucker's lessons on communications would prepare the largest newspaper on the West Coast to survive in an era when other newspapers were shuttering.

First thing that the publisher would need to do is to ask the editors what concerns they would have about the transition of print copy to web copy. Were there photography issues, how would word-count be affected? How would writers feel if their articles were web exclusive? The editors would take that information to their journalists and graphics departments, and then they would be able to report back what their concerns would be and, perhaps, what kind of additional staff may be required. The enthusiasm would have to be strongest from the top down because it would travel through several channels. This task would be repeated with their financial departments. The publisher would have to speak with web experts to understand how revenue can be charged, and, in order to create value, how the customer can track ROI.

The publisher would then have to approach the sales department, which accounts for nearly half of the newspaper's staff. This would include the marketing team, the display ad department, the classifieds department, real estate, automotive, etc. The publisher would have to address the concerns of the sales force which is charged with convincing customers to place ads on the internet version of the newspaper or to be marketed through phone apps. Perhaps the sales team may suggest that the new media might be confusing for a restaurant owner to understand. Perhaps a discount on print ads would be needed as an incentive. Perhaps, there were members of the sales team who just couldn't comprehend sizes, or features like flash, or placements on a page. These issues need to be addressed in order for the planned transition to succeed.

It is important for the executive to take this time to allow the sales team and the various marketing wings to have their concerns heard because, once they are addressed, the executive can shift the focus to the most important information of the communication, namely the meeting. What can be done? What needs to be done to make this happen, and how much time do we need to make this happen. It's very possible that they might have to revisit and constantly tweak the formula to successfully complete their transition to a web media empire, but if they tried to communicate from the top down they would have failed.

Communication is always reinventing itself, but certain core elements will always remain the same. One has to be constantly vigilant of making sure that the message gets across as cleanly and succinctly as possible. Follow the four essential steps to effective communication and you will have the best chance for success. Remember that communication is perception. Communication is expectations, and it always has to make demands. Always remember that Communication and information are different and, indeed, largely opposite–yet interdependent. Follow these steps and you will have a high chance for effective communication.

Relationship Management Challenge

All Work is Done Through Relationships

Relationship Management focuses on behavioral science, psychology, anthropology and interpersonal communication skills. It examines anticipated problems, interventions and resolutions of problems, and the ability to inspire and influence others and the capacity to communicate and build bonds with individuals to encourage change, growth, development and resolve conflict.

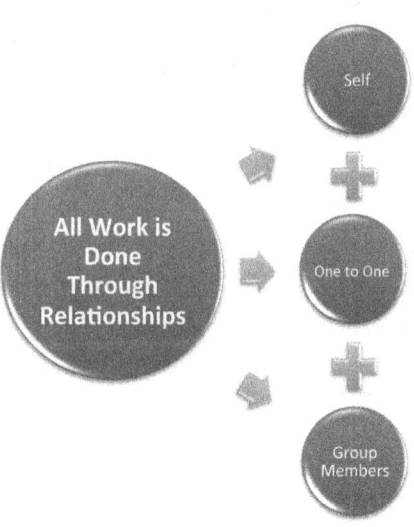

Self

Manager work to enhance the psychological knowledge and understanding of personnel so each individual becomes aware of themselves and their relationships with colleagues and upper management. Developing individuals' ability to manage themselves more effectively is an important component of co-workers fostering positive interpersonal relationships. Failure to successfully manage sensitivities complicates working relationships and impedes benefits to the organization.

One-to-One

Personal, one-to-one connections between individuals drive the initial interest and ultimate business engagements. The one to one business relationship acknowledges the realities of effective relationships and fits them together into opportunities that profit the company. Effective relationships in business require reciprocity, not a one way half hearted effort. Departments are more efficient and deliver greater outcomes for organizations to create unique experiences for workers to effectively build relationships that last.

Group Members

When groups or teams of diverse individuals are united together to work as one or to form a team, challenges such as communication, self awareness, emotional intelligence and relationship issues can result. The dynamic and complex nature of a group/team calls for a strong and decisive leader for continual guidance. Managers are required to evaluate potential challenges of group members/team development and create valuable ways to solve them before they happen. A supportive business environment helps workers to achieve greater productivity and efficiency.

Guynes's Concept on Basic Management

G Get
U Understanding
Y Your
N Needed
E Education
S Skills

Dr. Guynes's first suggestion on the *need to know* is as follows for example, desire and enthusiasm can be contagious when leading people in an organization. A manager should have the vision for the organization, should motivate and inspire top down. To be a gifted manager, one needs to know when to lead and when to follow via observation and feedback to improve the outcome. Guynes's second suggestion on the *need to know*: when do you know, who knows you, who should know what you are doing, how do I use what I know, when do I use or not to use what I know, how do I know what I know, how important is what I know, what is important in what I know to understand the need to know. I need to peruse, among others, as follow: strength, weakness, values, skills, right fit, commitment, healthy thinking, change, performing, engagement, challenges and goal setting for the future.

> *"Dr. Drucker's guidance and mentoring provided me the expertise to be a consultant."*
> –Dr. Luther Guynes, Ph.D.

3 Basic Approaches to Management

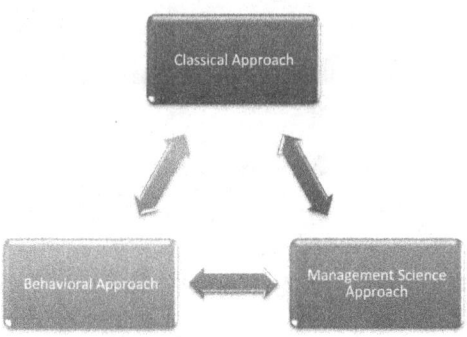

Classical Approach to Management:

Classical approach to management breaks job descriptions down into components which can be easily learned. Its goal is to maximize the efficiency of workers and thereby maximize productivity in the workplace. It relies on the development of a very specific job description for every employee. The classical approach to management is mainly concerned with increasing the efficiency of workers and organizations based on management practices, which are an outcome of careful observation and universal principles of operation in the striving for economic efficiency.

Behavioral Approach to Management:

Relies on the notion that managers will better understand the human aspect of workers and treat employees as an important asset to achieve organizational goals. Management taking a special interest in employees makes them feel like part of a special group. It establishes a work culture in which staff members feel valued and acknowledged, boosting employee motivation and empowering workers. The traditional authoritarian approach to leadership no longer yields the kind of results necessary for business success.

Scientific Approach to Management:

Visualizes management as a logical entity, the action of which can be expressed in terms of mathematical symbols, relationships, and the measurement of data. Through this device, managerial and other problems can be expressed and articulated in basic relationships and, where a given goal is required, the model can be expressed in terms which optimize that goal. This approach draws many things from the decision theory approach and, in fact, provides many techniques for rational decision making, systems analysis, and some aspects of human behavior.

> **Drucker's Wisdom**
>
> What information do I owe the people
> for whom I work and depend on?
> In what form and in what timeframe?

CHAPTER IV

SELF-ASSESSMENT

Drucker considered self-assessment as one of the most important steps toward moving a company forward. It is a method that is used to assess what you are doing as a company, why you are doing it, and what you need to do to improve overall performance. Proper self-assessment should ask these five essential questions: 1) What is our mission? 2) Who is our customer? 3) What does our customer value? 4) What are our results? 5) What is our plan? These are what Drucker referred to as the five most important questions you will ever ask about your organization.

Question 1: What is our Mission?
Drucker said that the first question you have to ask is: what is the mission of your company? This would include follow up questions, such as: what is your immediate mission? What sorts of challenges will you face as you attempt to complete the mission? What kinds of opportunities are available, and how will you react when they arrive? If you are failing to achieve the mission or straying from it, do you need to revisit your organization's mission? These fundamental questions need to be answered before you can go anywhere with your company.

An effective mission statement is short and sharply focused. It should fit on the front of a coffee mug. It answers the question why you do what you do. It doesn't say how you are going to set about doing it. The mission does not have to be specific, but it does have to direct you toward what you hope to accomplish in both the immediate and the distant future. It gives you a direction as an organization and it will be what guides all decisions throughout the company when it comes to reaching organizational goals. It must be clear and it must inspire. Drucker says that a proper mission statement should make every employee in the company think, "Yes, this is what I want to be remembered for."

To have an effective mission, you have to match your opportunities, competence and commitment. All effective mission statements reflect all three of these elements. Companies must aim their focus inward starting from the outside environment. If you work from the inside out, you may find yourself out of date and your resources unnecessarily eaten up. Demographics change, as do your customers' needs. You need to determine relevant information about what has already happened and seek out new opportunities for growth.

Successful leadership is able to anticipate the future and adapt to it. It is important to be able to grasp currents and future trends, but not to be so dependent on any time period that you fail to escape the trend after it has passed. A good company will always know where the opportunities lie and when to take them, and the mission should be flexible enough to adapt to these opportunities. In any event, opportunities should be tied into the core goal of staying close to the mission of the organization.

Drucker says to look keenly at changes within technology and the competitive environment. Look to the environment for available funding. Determine which gaps need to be filled. Things that are most important today may become the second or third most important within a relatively short time. In the blink of an eye, such a thing may even become completely irrelevant. You need to ask yourself where you can make the biggest differences imposed by the current limits of your human knowledge and financial resources. Where can you dig in and make a difference? Where can you raise the performance bar? What really motivates and inspires commitment to your goal?

Drucker made special note that one should "never subordinate the mission just for more money," because if you do this, then you will water down your mission. A non-profit that has a mission devoted to creating a voice for non-motorists in Los Angeles should never accept a corporate sponsorship from an automobile company, especially if it expects a return on their investment that doesn't synch with the company's mission. For example, if they expected the organization to promote a new Ford S.U.V., that would completely water down the mission. This happens often, so it is important to stick to your mission, even if it means passing on great financial benefit.

The mission should always be at the forefront of your thought process. Along the way, you will analyze challenges and opportunities, identify your customers, learn what they value, and write down and be honest when defining your results. Over time, as you formulate your plan, you will use self-assessment to affirm your mission or to accept that you may need to alter it. Ultimately, your mission statement won't define your organization so much as your personal performance does. Your mission is as strong as you are.

Question 2: Who is our customer?

To properly know what your mission is and how effectively your company accomplishes that mission, you need to ask yourself, "Who is our customer?" The actual answer is that there are both primary customers and supporting customers. While the primary customer is the top priority of a company, it cannot exist without successfully inspiring its supporting customers. These primary and supporting customers may swap spots over time, or you may find that people you never thought of as being your customer at all could suddenly become your primary customer. A smart organization knows who their primary and secondary customers are and sometimes, as changes in the environment happen, a mission may be modified to reflect those changes.

Drucker spent considerable time advising non-profits, which comprise the largest employment sector in the country. He would often use non-profits as surrogate organizations for the sake of his lessons. He discovered that many non-profits fail because they refuse to acknowledge their customers as customers. They felt that the term customer was a marketing term and something meant for commerce. They would often let their idealism blind them instead of taking a practical approach to managing their mission. They would often focus on the primary customer, while ignoring the secondary customers, or they would focus primarily on the secondary customer while neglecting their primary customer. Drucker was correct when he said that you had to sustain both your primary and secondary customers.

Drucker published the *Drucker Foundation Self-Assessment Tool* in 1999, and in it he describes a mid-sized non-profit with a mission to increase people's economic and social independence. For thirty-five years they had 25 programs, but they were entirely focused on one primary customer, the person with multiple barriers to employment. In the beginning, this meant strictly physically handicapped. Over time, however, the definition of the primary customer grew to include several different types of people: elderly, single mothers, recovering addicts, mentally ill, etc. Each of these separate groups now existed as part of the primary customer, those with multiple barriers to employment. Results are measured in all 25 programs based on whether the customer is afterwards able to secure and maintain employment.

Recognizing your primary customer will allow you to place your priorities in proper order and provide you a reference point to refer back to when trying to determine whether a program successfully focuses on the core mission.

Supporting customers are those who are not the sole focus of the organization, yet for a mission to succeed, they must also be nurtured and inspired. In a non-profit, that would include most of the employees, who work for wages that are typically low compared to the amount of work required. It would also include each member of a volunteer force. It includes those who contribute money on both monthly and annual bases. Supporting customers can even be people who may only give one or two times during their lifetime, but may leave an endowment in their will. It can be the neighborhood print shop that gives the non-profit a 10% discount every time they visit, saving hundreds or thousands of dollars annually. When telephone fundraisers call for donations and pass along front burner information, the recipients are secondary customers as well as everyone who receives a phone call after they fill out a form or visit a booth at some event. It is imperative that you take care of your secondary customers, but if you lose vision of who your primary customer is, you will never complete your vision, so don't get hyper-focused on your secondary customers, but also don't neglect them.

Your customers will always change and become ever more diverse. It is better to have your customer base grow than to have it shrink, so you have to take the time to nurture your customers and always stay aware of who they are, and who they are becoming. Customers will often be one step ahead of you, so you have to constantly reevaluate who your customers are. The customer base will always vary, but if you are able to maintain an understanding of your customers, you can specifically appeal to what your customer wants.

Question 3: What does the customer value?

When we ask what customers value, we are first trying to figure out what *we believe* our primary and supporting customers value; however, we need to ask *our customers* what they value. How do you do that? You have to figure out what kind of information you need to gain from your customers and then, of course, figure out how to obtain this important information.

The best way to find out what customers value is to go straight to the source, the customers themselves. Drucker warns against assuming that you know, especially if you are a top executive. It is far too easy to lose touch with your customers, but by taking steps as simple as making a series of phone calls or letters, or, these days, emails or survey apps, you can find out as accurately as possible directly what customers value, because they are telling you themselves.

Drucker pointed out that, all too often, organizations forget to ask what the customer values. He points out how often high-minded nonprofits tend to think too highly of their own view of what their customer values and don't bother asking. This neglect wastes company resources (customer feedback) and can potentially bottleneck the advancement of the mission. Don't confuse the institution as an end to itself. That is a wrong approach. It is a bureaucracy. Instead of asking if it fits your rules, focus on if it delivers a true value to your customers. If you mix those two points up, it will diminish the company vision. Understand your assumptions, but seek out what your customers want. Continue to assess your performance, and alter your approach as needed.

One simple way to assess what your primary customer values is by asking them directly. Often, an organization may be helping progress toward their mission's goals, but they may be missing out on a more efficient route because they don't understand the values of their primary customer. An example of that, which

Drucker used in his self-assessment tool workbook, referred to a nonprofit helping the homeless. The shelter valued providing the homeless meals and a warm place to spend the night. The primary customers, the homeless, appreciated the meals and the beds, but they placed a greater value on having an opportunity to get out of their homeless situations. When they had to leave first thing in the morning, if left them feeling they were unable to break out of their cycle of woe. Upon discovering this by interviewing their primary customers, the non-profit was able to revise their values to match those of their primary customers.

The shelter changed their focus beyond providing an overnight bed, and more on serving as a safe haven. They accomplished this by altering the way they ran the shelter, so that their primary customers were not forced to return to the streets during the day. Further, the non-profit created programs that would help the homeless residents find jobs and permanent housing. By adapting their approach and requiring more from and for their customers, it would bring results leading to better outcomes.

When it comes to your supportive customers, you really have to focus on why they support your organization. What inspires them? Drucker used the school model, in which a principal has students as the primary customer; however, they also have to address the values of their secondary customers, that of the parents, school boards, teachers and, in many cases, boosters and sponsors, that is, before you factor in the community. For the principal to just maintain his or her position or to excel, each group has to be satisfied as the principal steers clear of a mutiny among these possibly competing interests. The combination of these factors will determine how the curriculum is set, whether to focus on improving classwork or passing standardized tests, or even whether or not to have an athletic department or how much money and resources to devote to arts programs. If the principal fails to satisfy these many secondary customers while also meeting the needs of the primary customers, the students, the principal will ultimately fail, but principals who manage to satisfy all these customers' needs succeed, and will provide the institution with the best chance to achieve its mission.

Question 4: What are our results?

After you understand who your customers are and what they value, it is necessary to determine how successful you have been at satisfying your customers' values and completing the mission of the organization. Drucker said such an assessment should be done on a regular basis. In order to determine your results, you must first determine how to define the results. Once you have that defined, you need to determine if you are successful. Perhaps, you may be defining the results wrongly. Finally, you must determine what needs to be strengthened and what needs to be given up.

Say, for example, a preparatory academy is founded with the intention of better preparing high school graduates to succeed when they attend college. Their primary customers would be students who weren't quite prepared for college due to some academic or emotional reason. This would include students trying to level up in their college choices and student athletes who were preparing to receive athletic scholarships at colleges.

The first step that you could immediately look to is how successful you are at achieving your short-term goals. The clearest view of this is the college graduation rates of former students, five years removed and how many graduated. Since the mission is to assist students in achieving academic success at the next level, five years is the correct window to determine how that segment of the primary customer was served. The second step would be to look at college acceptances by the previous two classes of students who attended the academy with the intention of being accepted into a higher ranked institution than they would have been able to directly out of high school. The next step, if one wanted to probe deeper, would be to look at the data for student athletes who were offered athletic scholarships and see how many of those students graduated. After you are able to analyze the data, it can lead to long term change. For example, if one particular area of your primary customer group, be they athletes, level-uppers, or late-blooming students, achieves at a significantly higher rate than the others, you may want to readjust your focus. Determining your success at the short-term goals will impact how you move forward.

Progress and success can be appraised in qualitative and quantitative terms. When considered in combination, they shine a spotlight on how and where your organization is productive or deficient in achieving its organizational goals. Drucker defines qualitative measures as those which address the depth and breadth of a particular context, and quantitative measures as those identifying definite stages with hard data.

Qualitative measures begin with observations that reveal patterns. For example, an organization is unable to quantify the value of research ahead of time. Qualitative can begin with an outlier that later becomes a trend which can fall into a category of intangibles such as a hunch or instilling hope in a student's ability that they will figure out college algebra if that student maintains their efforts. Quantitative measures could show the student their progress not only compared to their previous work, but compared to previous students who followed similar trajectories. Both intuition and hard data must strike a balance.

Once you have the data, it is vital to determine what needs to be strengthened and what needs to be abandoned. Drucker states that no matter what changes one makes to a company, whether it is strengthening or eliminating, it must be guided by the mission of the organization. Many organizations are afraid to move onto anything that no longer works, is obsolete, or perhaps never even worked effectively. Don't be afraid to abandon something that doesn't work anymore or divert energy and resources from successful implementation of the organization's mission. Try something new that might be more effective, or devote all your resources towards the areas where your organization is showing strength and make it stronger.

As a rule, businesses and nonprofits resist change. It may go against how they were taught in college decades ago. It may be fear of the unknown. This may be a university dropping a particular language department or an organization updating their customer relation management (CRM) system. It could be a multi-media corporation selling off its broadcast radio entities. Change is good if it leads to strengthening the overall success of an organization's mission.

Finally, any decisions you make at this point in your company's self-assessment must be focused on the future success of the organization. You can look back, but don't live in the past. To be at the forefront, you have to take the best knowledge and embrace change. Establish yourself at the vanguard, not the rear. At the end of the day, top leadership must hold themselves accountable. Drucker stressed that leadership is ultimately held accountable for determining what needs to be done to protect the group from squandering resources and to ensure the most meaningful results.

Question 5: What is our plan?

After you have taken these steps, you need to ask yourself, "What is the plan for moving forward?" You need to decide whether or not the mission needs to be changed. You need to reassess what your goals are for the organization. After you do this, you will be ready to move your company forward.

Self-assessment should lead to a plan for the company that concisely summarizes the organization's purpose and future direction. It should encompass the organization's mission, vision, goals, objectives, action steps, a budget and an appraisal At this point you must decide whether to continue forward with the current mission or to adjust it. Then, apply long term goals. Drucker stressed that it has to answer the questions "What is our purpose?" Why do we do what we do?" "What, in the end, do we want to be remembered for?"

This provides the foundation for setting goals and for mobilizing the resources for the budget. Drucker stated that to further the mission there must be action today and specific aims for tomorrow. We need to work in both the short term and the long term. Limit your goals to no more than five. Anything more than five dilutes the mission. All future objectives must be measurable and concrete, and management must be responsible for these objectives since they are the knowledge workers. The five elements of effective plans are abandonment, concentration, innovation, risk taking, and analysis.

The plan begins with a mission and ends with action steps and a budget to pay for it. The action steps say who will do what and when, holding people accountable, and the budget determines what kinds of resources will be made available to achieve each step. Upon approval being affirmed by the governing body or board of your organization, the changes will be implemented immediately, or at some approved time. Never be satisfied with your plan, as it will always morph as will your customers and their values. By providing yourself with occasional assessment tests, you can maintain your organization's success at achieving their mission and expand the meaning of it at the same time.

Management Process and Organizational Objectives

The Management Process and Organizational Objectives work with and through others to effectively, efficiently, and ethically achieve organizational objectives in a changing environment. It is a social process involving the responsibility of effective planning by pursuing different functions of the management process.

> **Drucker's Wisdom**
>
> When focusing on the marketing for nonprofit institutions, focus only on the things that you are highly competent in. Stay in your lane. Do not neglect strategy.

CHAPTER V

NONPROFITS
Mission to Performance

The results of social sector organizations are always measured outside the organization in changed lives and changed conditions – in people's behavior, circumstances, health, hopes, and above all, in their competence and capacity. To further the mission, each nonprofit needs to determine what should be appraised and judged, then concentrate resources for results.
—**Peter Drucker**

Peter Drucker was an innovator when it came to consulting nonprofit agencies as businesses. For decades, nonprofits were seen as the opposite of business. The organizations took the term nonprofit literally and, without a business plan, many of those nonprofits lived up to the name and ceased operations. It was Drucker who realized that nonprofits are actually the largest sector of employers in the United States, with nearly one out of every two people contributing at least three hours a week at a nonprofit of some type. Drucker enjoyed consulting and studying nonprofits, and through his research and innovations, his lessons and theories still allow nonprofits to return their investment in improving and improved lives.

He realized that nonprofits need special attention because of the absence of a traditional bottom line since their mission is less about dollars and cents and more about lives improved. Drucker realized that unless nonprofits find a way to develop management skills as a tool to propel the institution, a nonprofit will drown in mismanagement. Part of the problem stemmed from the way management studies were geared specifically towards business bottom lines, so Drucker set about studying nonprofits and finding ways to make them better able to thrive.

Drucker recorded 25 cassette tapes of interviews with leaders at various nonprofits for an audio series entitled, *Leadership and Management in the Nonprofit Institutions*, also known as *The Non-Profit Drucker*. The series enjoyed enormous success when it was released in 1988. American and international nonprofits today still feel the impact. He intended these interviews to be listened to, rather than be read. Over time, however, listeners of the audio series and leaders of nonprofits repeatedly demanded a version in readable format. As a result, Drucker wrote and published the book *Managing the Nonprofit Organization Principle and Practices* in 1999. To this very day, both the book and the cassette series lay out a theoretical foundation and actionable plan for nonprofits to run proficiently.

Drucker recognized that, among employers and institutions, American nonprofits were a definite success of the latter half of the 20th century. He cited organizations such as *The American Heart Association* and *The American Cancer Society's* ability to make major medical breakthroughs in extending countless lives. He also cited civic-minded organizations like *The Girl Scouts of the U.S.A.* and *The Boy Scouts of the U.S.A*. At the turn of the 20th century, he claimed that the "non-profit sector has become America's 'Civil Society.'"

At the beginning of the 21st century, there were two primary challenges facing all non-profit organizations. They are the same two major challenges that all nonprofits must deal with: 1) how do you convert donors into regular contributors, and

2) how do you give the community a common purpose? By one measure or the other, these two challenges define and determine the success of most nonprofit organizations.

Nonprofits typically represent 2%-3% of the gross national product. This financial picture presents limitations in what nonprofits can effectively hope to forecast and what might be possible for them to achieve. One of the key difficulties faced by nonprofits is that they are competing with other nonprofits and charitable organizations, along with other political and lobbying organizations competing for the general public's allotted charitable giving. As the slices of the American GNP pie were realigned and divvied up, leisure more than doubled, and medical expenses skyrocketed, as did education and universities. Meanwhile, the overall percentage of national income devoted to nonprofits and charities remained stagnant through periods of economic growth and generational financial progress. It is not a given that the philanthropic leanings of an older generation will be passed on to future generations. Drucker recognized this as both a problem and an opportunity, and said, "we know that we can no longer hope to get money from 'donors;' they have to become 'contributors.'" He considered this to be the most urgent task for every single nonprofit.

Drucker approached the philanthropic nature of nonprofit organizations as a for-profit business would. He created the idea of selling self-realization through financial activism. In other words, rather than hoping to receive an annual end of the year holiday donation as tax deductible gifts, non-profits could inspire involvement by selling their customers the opportunity to give more money and time to create the change in the world that they themselves are unable to produce while working fifty hours a week as an accountant, a nurse or a teacher. It allows people to live out idealization of who they believe themselves to be. It allows people to feel a part of a cause larger than themselves. Nonprofits sell the moral conscience that allows ordinary people to look in the mirror and see the best version of themselves. Everyone wants to feel as if they are part of the solution and not part of the problem. By turning one-time or annual donors into frequent contributors, it is essential to sell the philanthropist on making an even greater difference by becoming a vital cog of a vital machine.

Even today, this impact of Drucker's work is enormously important to the industry. Secondary industries such as grant writers, telephone fundraiser lead generators, and parking lot petitioning companies have all evolved from this one innovation in philosophy. The innovation was simple. By constantly raising money, it serves the dual purpose of increasing the organization's revenue and increasing personal involvement through frequent contact with their customers, who are now active philanthropists.

The way the donor becomes a contributor is by maintaining a valued presence in the customer's lives. For example, a crisis is always a great reason to make additional contacts. A crisis depends on your organization's mission, but the crisis cannot be so specific and recent that appeals seem overly opportunistic. A good example of this is when UNICEF (United Nations International Children's Relief Fund) releases a report about death facing down starving and malnourished children. The report will typically appear far from the traditional giving season in late December–in the spring or in the summer. By releasing the report, UNICEF connects with concerned customers, who want to help ease the children's suffering. UNICEF follows up with an appeal for money. Three months later, they follow up with a phone call and ask if you have been reading about the crisis and then they ask for money again. Soon, their customers are well on their way to becoming contributors. Contributors are donors who have increased their annual giving by giving more often.

When they make the additional contribution, the organization provides them with a magazine subscription and, perhaps, a calendar or a stuffed toy. This works really well with animal nonprofits. The nonprofit encourages the philanthropist to read the literature provided and the donors begin to identify themselves with their affiliation with the organization that makes the world a better place. Ultimately, the goal of a manager in charge of fundraising is to turn every donor into a contributor and then finally into what is called a sustainer. Sustainers were less common during Drucker's days, but he would have definitely approved of the approach. Sustainers are contributors who make monthly contributions taken directly from their checking accounts. Sustainers are the new lifeblood for nonprofits.

Sustainers are so important these days for soliciting dependable income and encouraging active membership that organizations often fashion special marketing monikers for their sustainers–like Greenpeace's "Rainbow Warriors" or The Diane Fossey Gorilla Fund International calls their monthly sustainers the "Conservation Crew." These tags solidify the customer's satisfaction in such a way that their giving makes them feel as valued members of an international change-making organization. While the majority of Greenpeace's Rainbow Warriors won't be rappelling from corporate skyscrapers or hanging protest banners from oil riggers in the Arctic Ocean, donors, through their association made possible by monthly giving, rightfully feel a part of the team that makes this happen. They are tactfully reminded of their association via the subscriptions and associated stuffed toys and pledge pins. They take their persona into their meetings and they wear their idealism on themselves–literally. Meanwhile, nonprofits benefit by not only increasing their revenue but by showing predictable monthly and annual income streams, which they can now use for forecasts. An additional benefit of cultivating sustainer philanthropists is that many leave sizeable donations in their estate.

As for creating a common purpose for the community, Drucker pointed out that, while in the early 20th century, when many people left small farm towns for large and growing cities, they lost their deep connection to community. For example, in Los Angeles, there is a joke that say that nobody is actually from there; people move there. Further, even people in large cities have an intrinsic desire to belong to something that is a smaller community of their own. Often this need for connection can be filled by working as unpaid staff at a nonprofit organization. This benefits the customer by filling this void for community, while the organization benefits from the free labor, which ideally will push a group closer to meeting or exceeding their goals. For example, many of the volunteers at the Los Angeles County Bicycle Coalition, a nonprofit devoted to safe cycling in Los Angeles County, work full time jobs as attorneys and managers and teachers; however, they all contribute their valued time because it makes them feel part of a community. They are not compensated in dollars; they are being paid in the feeling of knowing they are a valued member of their community.

Drucker used to say the nonprofits are America's community. He believed the precise reason volunteers in nonprofits overachieve is because they are not being paid. For many people, working for one's self-satisfaction can carry far more of a different kind of value than pursuing the *almighty dollar* especially for people whose lifetime savings are tucked away in bank accounts. Drucker warned, however, that "precisely because volunteers do not have the satisfaction of a paycheck, they have to get more satisfaction out of their contribution. They have to be managed as unpaid staff." This is why Drucker devoted so much time toward the innovation of nonprofit management.

A mission should succinctly describe exactly what the nonprofit does as an organization and what the staff does when they come to work each day. It is the common goal that each person in the organization strives for, and individual goals all combine into the overarching nature of the mission. Nonprofits exist to create a change for the better in individuals and society. The real test goes beyond the eloquence of the mission statement. The real test is the action. As the leader of a nonprofit organization, your charisma is far less important than the leader's mission. So, the most important job of the leader is to define the mission of the organization.

Here are some examples of solid missions by currently successful, prominent nonprofits:

Greenpeace is an independent campaigning organization, which uses non-violent, creative confrontation to expose global environmental problems and to force the solutions essential to a green and peaceful future. **Greenpeace's** goal is to ensure the ability of the earth to nurture life in all its diversity.

The Southern Poverty Law Center is dedicated to fighting hate and bigotry and to seeking justice for society's most vulnerable. Through litigation, education, and other forms of advocacy, the **SPLC** works toward a day when the ideals of equal justice and equal opportunity will become a reality.

Amnesty International's mission is to undertake research and action focused on preventing and ending grave abuses of the rights to physical and mental integrity, freedom of conscience and expression, and freedom from discrimination, within the context of its work to promote all human rights.

UNICEF is mandated by the United Nations General Assembly to advocate for the protection of children's rights, to help meet their basic needs and to expand their opportunities to reach their full potential.

The Jimmy Fund solely supports the fight against cancer at Dana Farber. Since its founding in 1948, the **Jimmy Fund** has raised millions of dollars through thousands of community efforts to help save lives and give hope to cancer patients around the world.

Drucker used to refer to how most of the hospitals he visited would proclaim that their mission is "health care." This is not a mission. According to Drucker's lessons, a mission statement has to be operational. Otherwise, it's just a nice idea that lacks substance. The mission statement "has to focus on what the institution really tries to do and then does it, so that everybody in the organization can say, 'this is my contribution to the goal.'"

The job of the manager at the nonprofit is to convert the institution's mission statement into specific parts. Do not overload your mission statement. If you add something to your statement, a part of equal size should be removed. Note that in the above five mission statements, none of them exceed 50 words. Keep it simple. Your values statement can be longer, but the mission has to be succinct. Drucker used the success of fundamentalist colleges as an example of the success that comes from a narrow mission. People understand exactly what they are supporting when they attend a fundamentalist college. The teachers know, the parents know and, most importantly, the students understand that their emphasis will be on religion and not on the liberal arts.

When you create a mission, it is imperative that you focus on the strengths and on the performance. Whatever you excel at, do it better, especially if you are already going in the right direction. Never worry about being all things to all people, focus on what you do well and become the very best at it. If you are completely failing in an area, do not be afraid to abandon it. In fact, to abandon the pursuit of something you are no good at is one of the best things your institution can do, since you are now able to focus your resources (financial and human) toward things you do well, so the donations will receive a better return on investment (ROI.)

Determine where you as an organization can make the biggest difference, and with your limited (financial and human) resources, really raise the bar to a new level. Find ways in which you can make a serious difference. Then direct all your energy toward attaining that goal.

Know what you believe in, which should dovetail with your mission. If you believe in an unlimited right to bear arms, you will not make an effective manager for a nonprofit whose mission is to eliminate gun violence. Don't be impersonal with your mission. Anything done well has a team in which everybody is 100% committed. The higher the office, the higher the level of enthusiasm that should be expected, as excitement is the real trickle-down theory, especially in nonprofits. You need personal commitment to achieve organizational goals.

Remember that the mission takes precedence over leadership. Non-profit institutions exist solely for the sake of their mission. This has to always be at the forefront of the leadership's mind. It can never ever be forgotten or the organization can be set adrift. They exist to make a difference in society and in individuals. Always focus on the mission and revisit it from time to time as it is acceptable to revise the mission, but don't water it down to the point that it's useless. There should always be short-range goals that can be accomplished quickly, while also having long-range plans. Action is always short term, so you always have to ask yourself if this is the best use of your resources. Is the short-term gain here worth it in the larger vision? Leadership is always accountable for the results.

You want to be able to turn your idealism into positive results. Nonprofits don't merely deliver a product or a service to its customers. As Drucker noted, nonprofits "want the end-user not to be a user, but a doer." The service is a call to action. The results are better community, but the service is a call to become active. To run a successful nonprofit it is essential that you have these four elements in place quickly: 1) a plan, 2) marketing, 3) people, and 4) money.

For many decades, successful nonprofits believed that they didn't have to resort to marketing, as that was a term used in a for-profit business model. They relied on the old methods of holiday time charity and tax deduction donations. Marketing, however, is enormously beneficial to nonprofits. It is in the approach. You are appealing to the heart strings of the soul. You are not selling a toaster. It is vital to understand your philanthropical customers. Rely on customer research.

Drucker admired the marketing of The American Cancer Society. Their stated mission:

> *The American Cancer Society is the nationwide community-based voluntary health organization dedicated to eliminating cancer as a major health problem by preventing cancer, saving lives, and diminishing suffering from cancer, through research, education, advocacy, and service.*
> *No matter who you are, we can help.*

He described The American Cancer Society's elaborate marketing research, which included detailed census data for fundraising. They used a network of physician advisory committees to communicate directly with physicians. Reaching out to physicians was extremely important, since they are the person who makes the direct referrals to the patients, so the physicians are technically the top customers of the advisory committees. In the 21st century, these innovations that Drucker marveled at in the 1980s is now commonplace in phone banks across the country. Even today, though, The American Cancer Society is one of the major innovators in marketing and motivating its base.

When focusing on the marketing for your nonprofit institution, only focus on the things that you are highly competent in. Stay in your lane. In your marketing, you want to have your true strengths. A typical appeal would be an introduction, a problem, a solution, and an appeal. You want to be associated with the places where you can make a change. If your organization focuses on the safety of redwood trees, don't waste your marketing talk about issues that are not related to saving redwood trees. Also, know your customers. For example, if you are running a nonprofit like Environment America, which is trying to prevent greenhouse gasses from destroying the climate, you would not want to waste your marketing dollars focusing on conservative Republican-leaning regions of the country where their elected officials do not believe in climate change. Know who your customers are and appeal to them full force.

When it comes to raising funds, your first constituency will be your board. Your board cannot just be in sympathy with the mission, they have to be highly passionate about the cause. However, you do have to have some people on the board who hold down the business end as well. There needs to be a balance between your resources and your effectiveness. The board is the guardian of the trust which holds the money for the nonprofit. The board makes sure that the funds are used to pay for the programs they were intended for. You need the highest quality people on your board who can help develop your base of donors, contributors and volunteers by providing example and leadership.

In order to have a successful nonprofit, you have to employ a winning strategy. Before you can do that however, you need to have a strategy. Strategies are action focused. You work for a strategy to be successful. You need to work smarter and the best way to do that is by placing them in the positions where they are most likely to produce the greatest results. Constant improvement also includes abandoning whatever things no longer or never worked. Find the areas where you can make a marked improvement. **Vision Zero** is a nonprofit devoted to street safety for pedestrians and bicyclists. Their mission statement:

> *"The primary mission of government is to protect the public. ... This **Vision Zero** Action Plan is the City's foundation for ending traffic deaths and injuries on our streets. The City will use every tool at its disposal to improve the safety of our streets."*

Vision Zero relies on data they release in annual reports in each city showing how their program is improving its ROI in lives saved and pedestrian-automobile collisions prevented.

You need to know what type of results you want so that way you know which data will benefit you in your quest toward improving society through your institution. Your goal has to fit your mission, and so the results need to coincide with that as well. For example, Vision Zero could set a one-year goal to reduce pedestrian collisions in front of schools, hospitals, and senior centers. This can all be measured, and it all fits within the core of the institution's mission to end traffic deaths. When they look at the statistics one and two years down the road, they will know exactly how successful they were at reducing those collisions.

Next, you need a marketing plan. For each targeting group, you will need a marketing effort. How will you reach out to each segment? You also need a way to recruit money and people into the program. You have to be able to communicate to everyone, who needs to do what, and what they need to reach the expected and necessary goals. You will need to train with your team a lot. You need to know what sort of supplies and resources will be needed. Most importantly, you need to set a defined date to see the results. For Vision Zero, it is the yearly data reports.

When you create the strategy and the goals, you should communicate the final program to the staff in both written and oral form. By writing it out, everyone has a copy of what the team goal is and how their work contributes to that end. It tells them what is expected of the management and what is expected by the individual performers. Finally, it says how and when their performance will be measured. The oral form can come in the form of a staff meeting. This is an opportunity to hash out any questions or concerns of any of the team members. At the meeting, provide all the team members with the printed version of the strategy. There is no perfect go-to winning strategy, but the one thing that Drucker stressed to not ever do on a strategy is to avoid defining your goals to steer clear of controversy. Never compromise on your goals.

Drucker said,

> *"Strategy converts a nonprofit institution's mission and objectives into performance."*

Do not neglect strategy. Strategy ends with a selling effort, but it begins with understanding your market, your customers, their needs and their expectations. A marketing strategy for a nonprofit institution needs to integrate the mission with the customer. Then, use the strategy to build its donor base and develop those donors into contributors and a higher level of contributor on a "partner" level. All strategies begin with research. Know where you are going and what you are doing. Train your employees, but you also need to have an understanding of how to train your volunteers. Volunteers are often your public face. Everyone needs to conform. Enthusiasm comes top down from the officers. Be committed as an organization to abandoning whatever does not work.

Strategy begins with a mission, and it ends with a work plan. Strategy commits the non-profit executive and the organization to action. It interweaves mission, objectives, the market and opportunity. The tests of strategies begin with needs and end with satisfactions for nonprofit organizations. Your satisfaction should be your customers' satisfaction. Nonprofit executives need to understand and respect their donors, volunteers and customers enough to listen to their values and become aware of their satisfactions. That is the only way they will know how effective they are as an institution.

Quadrants of Organizational Effectiveness

Organizational Capacity

Organizational capacity refers to an organization's potential to organize their human, financial and other resources to effect positive change. Organizational capacity is impacted by a myriad of factors, including the organization's stage of development, leadership and changes in the environment. Organizations engage in capacity building actions in order to enhance their effectiveness in serving their constituency. Such actions include, but are not limited to, hiring new employees to meet increased demand for services; strategic planning to position themselves for changes in the environment; training staff and management on roles and responsibilities, and automating financial systems.

Organizational Outcomes

Successful organizations require a culmination or inspirational leaders, sound managers, emotional balanced employees, and personal and social competence among all staff which is a key component of any healthy organization. Achieving emotional balance in the midst of our chaotic society is becoming increasingly important in our changing economy. In order to achieve increase and sustainable outcomes, organizations need to execute strategies, and express compassion in order to employ long term personal success with employees. Organizational outcomes are measured by analyzing where the organization is in regards to its goals and its forecasted mission.

Program Capacity

Program capacity is the process in which an organization improves, retains, obtains, and maintains the knowledge, tools, skills, equipment and other tangible and intangible resources required to do their job competently. Effective methods of management and revenue control are also used to handle the problems associated with organizational, and economic transformations. Program capacity also focuses on understanding the obstacles the organization faces in realizing their development goals and enhancing the company's ability to achieve measurable and sustainable results.

Program Outcomes

Organizational outcomes are critical to success in any thriving economy. In order to achieve increased and sustainable business results, organizations need to execute strategy and engage organized employees. All elements must be working together toward the same common goal in order to get strategy execution right. These elements work together, mutually reinforcing each other, and must be focused and aligned to effectively achieve execution. Effective strategy execution is paramount to an organizations success. There are challenges, but knowledge, strategy, focus, and an integrated approach can ensure the business survives and thrives under all economic conditions.

> **Drucker's Wisdom**
>
> Efficiency is doing the right thing.
> Effectiveness is doing the right thing right.

CHAPTER VI

LEADERSHIP

Drucker interviewed and consulted with top executives at some of the most successful American and international corporations of his day, as well as the most successful and most highly regarded non-profit institutions. He paid attention to the habits and the practices of these top executives. He took notes and observed similarities that carried over to most, if not all, of the executives. Drucker saw **eight essential practices** that were characteristic of the most effective leaders. He observed:

1. They asked, "What needs to be done?"
2. They asked, "What is right for the enterprise?"
3. They developed action plans.
4. They took responsibility for decisions.
5. They took responsibility for communications.
6. They focused on opportunities rather than problems.
7. They ran productive meetings.
8. They expressed the corporate needs in terms of "We" rather than in terms of "I."

The first two practices ensured that they understood what needed to be done and why. The next four steps allowed them to translate that knowledge into a successful action plan. The final two practices made the organization's mission a team effort and not the individual mission of a top leader. To succeed, everything has to be a team effort, but the greatest level of passion and organization needs to be focused in the top office.

When looking at failing companies or failing organizations, it is fairly easy to see, which of these eight elements are being ignored. If a top executive is skipping any of these steps, they will likely not succeed, but if they do succeed, it is probably more due to external factors than to their leadership. While a broken clock is correct twice a day, a broken leader is never so fortunate. These errors are often the simplest to repair; however, one must be honest with themselves to make the change.

The top executive needs to know more than anyone else in the organization what needs to be done and how the team will set about making this happen. With a nonprofit, they must know everything about the mission. With a corporation, they must be experts in the product they sell. Traditionally, in a sales organization, the CEO or the top sales executive has the final word when closing a top sale. For example, the CEO of a media entity won't sit through every advertising meeting with every client running a couple of thousand dollars a month in media placements; however, if there is an opportunity to sign a multimillion-dollar deal, with a company of equal or larger size, the CEO or publisher will be brought in for the closing meetings and for the contract signing. Aside from the respect implied by bringing a figurehead to the contract table to avert a potential crisis in the event of last-second negotiations that may torpedo the deal, it is acknowledged that the ultimate expert and the ultimate authority are the same person.

On the other hand, if the top executive doesn't understand what needs to be done and why, they can hardly inspire a team of workers to expend faithful obedience to a cause. If the leader of a media company doesn't fully understand web media, yet is ordering the sales staff to prioritize web sales over print sales, the executive will be unable to successfully motivate the staff. Instead, the staff will become confused and even stagnant, as they want to make sales, but they don't want to sell the wrong product. Many on the team will have questions and, if the top executives are not properly prepared to address the workers' concerns, the employees may become restless, rather than excited to undertake the new task.

Ask yourself, "What do I need?" One of the great mistakes made by incoming top executives is that they focus on what they want to do rather than on what needs to be done. The first question any top executive needs to ask themselves is: What needs to be done? Drucker used an example of Jack Welch, former CEO of General Electric (1981-2001).

> "Jack Welch realized that what needed to be done at General Electric when he took over as chief executive was not the overseas expansion he wanted to launch. It was getting rid of GE businesses that, no matter how profitable, could not be number one or number two in their industries."

It's worth noting that during Welch's two decades as CEO, General Electric's value increased by a whopping 4,000 percent. His work was so greatly appreciated by General Electric that, when he retired, he received a severance package exceeding $400 million, the largest corporate severance package in history. By focusing only on businesses which General Electric could be the very best at and not on his preferred overseas expansion, Welch will likely be forever remembered as one of the greatest CEOs in the history of corporate America. He saw what needed to be done, and focused on it.

The most effective leaders do not spread themselves out too thinly by branching out their main focus. Ideally, they focus on one primary task at hand. Two tasks can work for people who need to break up their day. However, a top executive should never extend themselves beyond that. Therefore, after asking what needs to be done, the effective executive sets priorities and sticks to them. All the secondary tasks, no matter how important or appealing, have to be set aside. However, after the original top-priority task has been completed, the efficient executive leader resets priorities rather than mechanically going on to whatever task was number two from the original list. The best leaders will ask themselves: What must be done now? Typically, this will result in newer and more pressing priorities. And those move up to the top of the list. If a top executive fails to focus on what needs to be done now, rather than what is listed as the number two task on their original list, they will find themselves falling behind the times and they will lose their relevancy before they have an opportunity to catch up.

Drucker referred to Welch's thought processes, as he had great respect for his proficiency, which was perhaps only rivaled by Alfred Sloan of General Motors, whom Drucker spent an entire year observing during the 1940s. Every five years Welch would ask himself what needed to be done now, and famously every time he would ask himself that question, he would conclude his thoughts with a new top priority. Welch would also think through another issue before making his decision where to concentrate his efforts for the next half-decade. He always asked himself which of the two or three tasks at the top of his list would he himself be best suited to undertake. Then he would direct his energies toward completing that task; the others he delegated. Effective executives should only focus on jobs they know they'll do especially well. They know that institutions succeed if top management performs—and they fail if it doesn't.

The second practice that all effective executives use to lead and which has to be adopted as entirely as the first practice is to ask: Is this the right thing for the enterprise? They know that shareholders, employees, and executives are important constituencies who have to support a decision, or at least acquiesce in it, if the choice is to be effective. But they also know that a decision that isn't right for the enterprise will ultimately not be right for any of the stakeholders. In the instance of a nonprofit, this will be focused on the mission of the organization. In those cases, they will likely be dealing with a board that controls the institution's funds, preserved in a trust. They will have to appeal to the board in those cases, but as with business enterprises, the focus must be on the mission, and if it isn't, then it is not likely that the board will approve it anyway.

Drucker pointed out the failure of nepotism, for example. Nepotism is promoting a family member or a close friend to a position of power they are not qualified for. This immediately brings up concerns by employees regarding the company's ethics as it pertains to advancement in the company. Ethics, in this case, are the principles that define right, good, and proper behavior and that draw a line between right and wrong. By placing an unqualified manager or executive into a leadership position, not only will the subordinates' morale decline, but department production will decline as well, because the staff will be forced to accommodate an unqualified leader to the probable detriment of their assigned work. These leaks may then drip down and corrode the entire chain. Leaders have to be qualified and lead by performance. In family-run corporations, only promote relatives when their promotion is merit based. Asking "What is right for the enterprise?" Will never guarantee that correct decisions will be made. Even the most genius executive is human, not a machine. Therefore, even the greatest leaders are prone to mistakes and prejudices. But failure to ask the question virtually guarantees the wrong decision.

Drucker always said that "Executives are doers." They are less concerned with collecting information than they are with completing tasks. However, executives can't just dive in blindly. First, they must plan his or her course. The effective leader needs to think about desired results, probable restraints, future revisions, check-in points, and implications for how they'll utilize their available time.

An effective action plan focuses on areas where the top executive can orchestrate the greatest positive change for the corporation or institution. Drucker suggests the first questions asked before going active is: What contributions should the enterprise expect from me over the next 18 months to two years? What results will I commit to? What are my deadlines? Then he considers the restraints on action: Is this approach legal and ethical? Is this compatible with the organization's mission values and policies? Will this be acceptable within the organization? Affirmative answers do not guarantee that an action will be effective.

Drucker preferred an action plan that is a statement of intentions rather than a commitment. Intentions are elastic and they should not restrict the company from making better decisions as future opportunities arise. A written plan should anticipate the need for flexibility. There needs to be a method for checking the effectiveness of how the plan is working. Once or twice a year should be effective. You can't be afraid to make adjustments when you see what is and is not working. It is not a flaw for a leader to eliminate something not working. It is a necessity that keeps the company growing upward, much like trimming hedges. Ultimately, the action plan will become the basis for the effective leader's time management. Time is an executive's most valuable resource and it is also their rarest commodity. Drucker adroitly emphasized that, "The action plan will prove useless unless it's allowed to determine how the executive spends his or her time."

Drucker emphasized that when effective leaders translate their plans into action, they must pay particular attention to their decision making, communicating, and any opportunities that may arise. They should also make sure that any meetings have a purpose that leads to their desired goals. It is also essential that any leader take responsibility for their decisions. Do not be a finger pointer if things go bad.

A decision has not been made until people know who is accountable for carrying it out. There needs to be a clear and defined deadline. There is a need to know who will be affected by the decision, and therefore, have to know about, understand, and approve it. At the very least, they can't be strongly opposed to it. Finally, a decision has not been made without an awareness of those who have to be informed of the decision, even if they are not directly affected by it.

Some of the trickiest decisions will be ones that regard hiring and firing. It is proven that only a third of all hiring falls into the "successful" category. Nearly an equal amount of hiring will fall into unsuccessful categories, while the remaining third fall into the merely adequate hiring categories. Calendar reviews are thereby essential to determine which category each new hire falls into. If a mistake is made, rectify it. However, the leader has to own all decisions and thus the mistakes as well. In a well-managed enterprise, it is understood that people who fail in a new job, especially after a promotion, may not be the ones to blame.

Excellent leaders owe it to their organization as well as to their fellow team members to not tolerate underachieving performers who hold important positions. It may not be the fault of the employees that they are not performing at the required level but, regardless, they must be eliminated. A systematic decision review can be a powerful tool for self-development as well.

Checking the results of a decision against its expectations shows leaders what their top skills are, areas they may need to improve, and where they are not equipped with the proper knowledge. Systematic decision review also shows executives the areas in which they are simply incompetent. In these areas of lesser competence, smart executives delegate their actions to someone they trust is better equipped to perform that task. Drucker always asserted that "There is no such thing as a universal executive genius." Making the best decisions is an imperative skill at all levels. It needs to be made crystal clear to everyone in institutions that are knowledge-based.

An effective leader needs to take responsibility for communicating. It is their responsibility to be understood. The effective leader needs to ask each level of employee what needs to be done and what tools are necessary in order for the task to be completed. When it comes to communicating through an entire company, the information flow from subordinate to boss is usually what gets the most attention. Rely on regional managers and floor managers to be emissaries between the assembly line workers and the executives. If the task is not understood, it will never be completed.

Drucker always emphasized that the best leaders are ones who focus on opportunities rather than problems. They take smart chances, when the odds are in their favor, because of their expertise or position. Drucker suggests that effective leaders should always ask themselves, "How can we exploit this change as an opportunity for our enterprise?"

Drucker singled out **seven specific types of opportunities** worth exploring:
1. an unexpected success or failure in their own enterprise, in a competing enterprise, or in the industry
2. a gap between what is and what could be in a market, process, product, or service (for example, in the 19th century, the paper industry concentrated on the

10% of each tree that became wood pulp and totally neglected the possibilities in the remaining 90%, which became waste)
3. innovation in a process, product, or service, whether inside or outside the enterprise or its industry
4. changes in industry structure and market structure
5. demographics
6. changes in mind-set, values, perception, mood, or meaning
7. new knowledge or new technology.

Drucker emphasizes opportunities rather than problems. He states further that the opportunities should be on page 1 of reports, while problems should be relegated to page 2. He also suggests leaving problems out of opportunity meetings with the exception of catastrophic emergencies that cannot be delayed. When it comes to staffing, effective leaders put their best people on opportunities rather than on problems. Drucker spoke of great leaders making occasional lists of their company's greatest opportunities and a second list of their greatest employees. Then the executive leadership would discuss and find ways to mesh the two lists together so that their best people were focused on the greatest opportunities for the company or the nonprofit to grow and complete their mission.

All good leaders absolutely require that any meetings they order be productive. Effective leaders understand the difference between work sessions and friendly bull sessions and they don't waste time. They don't have the time to waste. Time is their most valuable resource. Even if the meeting is scheduled for one-on-one, there needs to be a purpose for it. Drucker relayed an anecdote of one-time CEO of General Motors, Alfred Sloan (1923-1956):

"Sloan, who headed General Motors from the 1920s until the 1950s, spent most of his six working days a week in meetings–three days a week in formal committee meetings with a set membership, the other three days in ad hoc meetings with individual GM executives or with a small group of executives. At the beginning of a formal meeting, Sloan announced the meeting's purpose. Then he listened. He never took notes and rarely spoke except to clarify a confusing point. At the end, he summed up, thanked the participants and left. Then he immediately wrote a short memo addressed to one attendee of the meeting. In that note, he summarized the discussion and its conclusions and spelled out any work assignment decided upon in the meeting (including a decision to hold another meeting on the subject or to study an issue). He specified the deadline and the executive to be accountable for the assignment. He sent a copy of the memo to everyone present at the meeting. It was through these memos–each a small masterpiece–that Sloan made himself into an outstanding effective executive."

The best leaders always understand that every meeting is either productive or pointless.

Finally, it is important that you don't speak in the first person singular when discussing team goals. Never say "I"; always say "We." The best leaders know they have the final word on everything, and that they are the least replaceable member of the team, but they only have the power within the organization because the people in the organization trust him or her with the authority. They need to think and say "We" and always put the organization first.

The one thing that all great leaders have in common is they get the right tasks completed. Some are born effective. But the demand is much too great to be completed by raw talent. Drucker described effective leadership as a discipline that can be learned but must be earned.

Management and Organization Resources

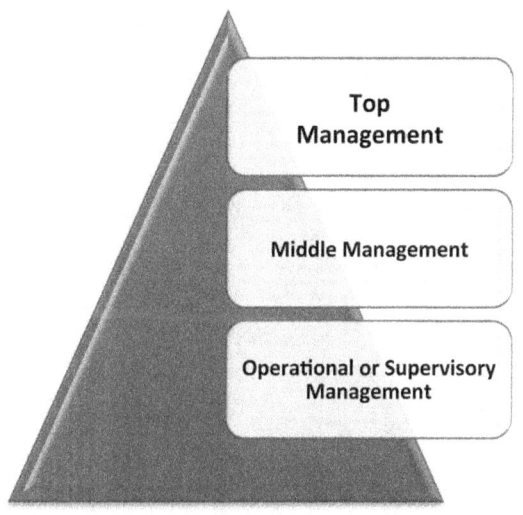

Top Management

The top level managers/executives are ultimately responsible for the entire organization. The top level management includes top executives such as chief executive officer (CEO), chairman of the board of directors, president, executive vice-presidents and various vice-presidents.

Middle Management

The middle management level generally consists of divisional and departmental heads such as plant managers, production managers, marketing managers, personnel directors and so on. Their responsibility is to interpret policies and directions set by the top level management into specific plans and guidelines. Responsibilities further include coordinating the working of their departments so that the set objectives can be achieved. They are concerned with short-term goals, divisional activities and specific results.

Operational or Supervisory Management

This level of management consists of supervisors, superintendents, unit heads, foremen, chief clerks and so on. The primary concern of the first level managers is with the mechanics of the job and they are responsible for coordinating the work of their employees.

They must possess technical skills so that they can assist their subordinate workers where necessary. Their responsibilities are inclusive of plan day-to-day operations, oversee activities, assign workforce to specific jobs, evaluate staff performances and are a link between the workers and the middle level management.

Skills Needed for Management Levels

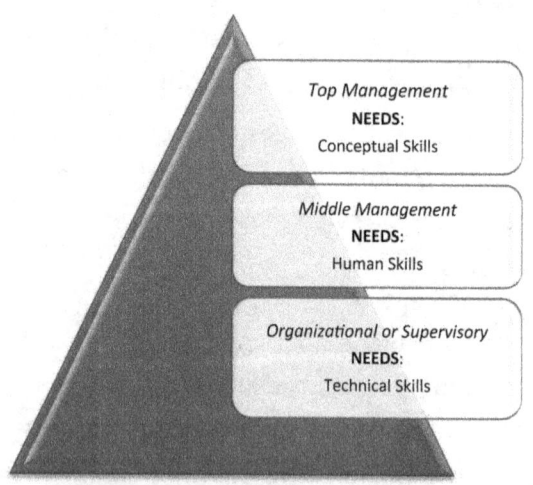

Needs of Top Management–Conceptual Skills

These skills assist top management to see how all the parts of an organization work together to achieve the organization's goals and objectives. Individuals with conceptual skills are creative and can navigate through abstract concepts and ideas. Conceptual skills are extremely important for leadership positions, particularly upper and middle management positions. Managers need to make sure everyone working for them is helping to achieve the company's larger goals.

Top 5 Conceptual Skills
- Strong Communication Skills
- Analyze and Evaluate
- Creative Thinking
- Strong Leadership Skills
- Problem Solving

Needs of Middle Management—Human Skills

In an evolving business world candidates are now sought after in several different ways. No longer does an employer know about a candidate simply from an emailed resume. Social media, job search profiles, college fairs, and filling out information from a career portal page, and so on are popular alternate sources. Employers are scouting for more than book knowledge. You can be the smartest person in your class, and have zero human skills or "common knowledge." In the workplace human skills can be just as important as work skills because people are constantly interacting with others from many different cultures. The most important skills in today's workforce are:

Essential Human Skills
- Adaptability
- Interpersonal Skills
- Effective Communication
- Learning—Ability to learn quickly and efficiently

Organizational or Supervisory NEEDS–Technical Skills

At the bottom of the managerial hierarchy, is the lower management group called supervisory management consisting of supervisors or foremen and office superintendents. It is the lower management group responsible for implementing the plans of management into effective action, allocating individual work and overseeing the accomplishment and fulfillment of the organization. This level determines the objectives of the business as a whole and executes policies to achieve these objectives by making and providing guidelines for actions and diverse decisions.

> **Drucker's Wisdom**
>
> Innovation is an important asset to companies that rely on strength for success. The time to make positive changes or to use innovation is when the company is at the top of their field.

CHAPTER VII

SUCCESS THROUGH STRENGTH

"Effective executives know that their subordinates are paid to perform and not to please their superiors. They know that it does not matter how many tantrums a prima donna throws as long as she brings in the customers. The opera manager is paid after all for putting up with the prima donna's tantrums if that is her way to achieve excellence in performance."
–Peter Drucker, *The Effective Executive*

Effective executives always rely on their strengths to succeed. That is a staple of all lessons taught by Drucker, and it was a central element of all of his consultations, whether it was to nonprofits, international corporations, or political party leaders. It is based on the idea that one cannot build on weakness. If you don't lead through your strengths by making your strength even stronger then you will most likely fail as an effective leader. You don't advance a corporation by worrying about what you can't do. Drucker always said to recognize what you can do and where you perform the best, and to strive to make yourself even better in that area, and use that as your calling card for success.

When it comes to strengths, Drucker wasn't only referring to the strengths of the top executive's strengths. He was also referring to the strengths of everyone within the organization, including those of their associates and those of their subordinates. These strengths need to be recognized as the opportunities to build, and it is the organization's job to maximize these strength-driven opportunities. The ideal goal is using the strengths of each team member as the basis for joint performance.

This strength-based performance should begin with your staffing decisions. An effective top executive will recognize the strengths of each staff member they hire, and they will be placed in a position to develop their strengths to fullest capacity. Effective leaders fill their positions by determining who can succeed at taking advantage of the organization's strengths. They don't focus on shoring up areas of weakness. They focus on performing so well at what they are strong at that it will in theory make up for any other shortcomings in other areas. Strong leaders never choose staff for the purpose of minimizing weaknesses but, rather, for maximizing strengths.

Drucker often made reference to one of his personal management heroes, Alfred P. Sloan Jr., who headed General Motors for four decades during the first half of the 20th century (1920s through 1950s). At the time of his chairmanship, he was probably one of the five most successful CEOs in the country. Yet, he would hand-select each individual GM executive from the Chief Operating Officer, "down to the manufacturing managers, controllers, engineering managers, and master mechanics and even the tiniest of accessory divisions." His only concern was for their performance at the corporation. Sloan's long-term performance was absolutely legendary when it came to placing the right people in the correct positions to capitalize on their individual and combined strengths for the company.

A conservative choice to avoid failure will always end in disappointment. Be bold with your staffing. Whoever tries to place a manager or staff an organization with the intention of avoiding weakness will end up at best with mediocrity. Drucker strongly dissuaded top executives from seeking out the so called "Jack of all trades" type of executive, because you wind up with an office full of utility players while being completely devoid of experts. Drucker has zero notions about the mythological super-executives who possess only strengths and zero weaknesses. Rather, Drucker pointed out that most of the top experts have limited areas at which they excel at an elite level, and that they also have equally large blind spots or weaknesses. The key to successfully building a powerful corporation is to staff the areas where you as the top executive are weak with employees who are expert at those positions. That way, you can focus on the area where you are skilled.

Any top executive who worries about what an employee can't do rather than with what they can do, and who, as a result, actually avoids weakness rather than making their strength effective is a weak leader themselves. In fact, it is likely that the poorly staffing executive may be intimidated by a subordinate's strengths–another sign of weakness.

A human excels in relating perception to action and works best if the entire person, muscles, senses and mind is engaged by the work. While work is therefore best laid out as uniform, working is best organized with a considerable degree of diversity. Work is an extension of personality and it is one of the most characteristic ways that people tend to define themselves. It is the way that people measure up to fellow peers in their field of practice. All work is a service and deserving of respect. Especially, if you place knowledge experts in their positions of expertise and strength, you will find that you have a highly proficient organization.

One of the best ways to bring out the most in people's individual strengths is by bonding them together by a sense of community. The classic television show "The Office" showed off the simple fact of human nature that Drucker was keenly aware of.

An office or warehouse or plant often acts as a surrogate home and provides the only sense of community that many employees have in their lives. By playing to the sense of community, you can instill additional pride in employees for their exclusive knowledge which they alone contribute to their micro-community. The accountant will take great pride in discovering loopholes which save the team money. The sales executive will take pride in bringing home the last sale on the final day of the month to reclaim a Salesperson of the Month award, the graphic designer will find a way through their creative knowledge to make a beautiful advertising campaign which increases the sale of the product 15% over the previous year. Creating contests among the staff which incorporates a team goal and a team reward is also a great way to use the power of community to enhance the powers of the teams' combined strengths to get the job done.

Strong leaders don't worry about whether or not their employees or subordinates like them. They concern themselves with whether or not the employee is properly completing assigned work. They ask how that member contributes to the team. They focus on their strengths, rather than their shortcomings. Strong leaders focus their hiring on applicants with one outstandingly strong skill, rather than the utility player who does everything pretty good, but nothing great.

The perfect example to explain this practice is the legendary NFL football mind, Bill Belichick. Drucker would often compare the great business leaders to great generals, and the one example in post-millennial leadership who combines both these elements is NFL Head Coach Bill Belichick. The modern NFL is a hybrid of war and business. It is the ultimate combat collision sport, watched by hundreds of millions around the world. It is also run by a conglomerate of team owners, made up of some of the wealthiest and most successful executives in the world. An average team costs billions of dollars and generates hundreds of millions of dollars annually. The average team employs its hierarchy of front office, field level management, positional coordinators, and the reliance on constant staffing to incorporate the necessary innovation to maintain the pinnacle of its profession. The NFL is very much in line with Drucker philosophies. In fact, most likely the majority of team owners, if not all of them, have probably read several of Drucker's lessons. After all, owning an NFL team is the ultimate prize for the highest-level businessmen, since there are only 32 available.

Belichick has been the head coach of the New England Patriots since the year 2000, and has made a specialty of filling his roster with players who excel at specific individual aspects of the game, rather than employing the traditional players who are adequate at everything. Belichick is widely regarded as the greatest head coach in modern football history, if not the greatest modern coach in all professional sports. Since taking over as the top executive for the Patriots, he has broken virtually every record for success and sustained success, such as most Super Bowl victories, most Super Bowl appearances, most all-time playoff victories, most regular season victories since the turn of the century and most consecutive division championships, among other outstanding accomplishments.

Belichick has famously always been able to fill his roster with less glamorous players who possess one extraordinary skill essential to winning games. A majority of the players are former cast offs from previous employers, because their previous teams felt they were too one-dimensional. In Drucker language, the general managers of the other teams are focusing on what quality contributors cannot do well, instead of prioritizing what they do extremely well. As a result, he has a deeper team, and every player knows that their job is to do their job. As a result, the Patriots traditionally have a team with the greatest number of team members who play on any given day. Every player participates and does their job, and they focus on making each player's strengths even stronger, while allowing another player to focus on an area of Player A's weakness. That way, whenever Player A is in the game, he is able to perform not only as a "specialist," but he will actually be performing as an elite specialist.

Innovation is an important asset to companies that rely on strength for success because the time to make positive changes or innovations is when the organization is at the top of their field. If you hesitate and follow a risk-averse approach to innovation (*e.g.*, advances in technology) until your competition successfully applies it, you may find yourself passed over by the savvier competitor who will emerge at the top of the field. Drucker was insistent in the way he defined innovation, and he categorized the willingness to apply innovative approaches to running a business as a great strength for a leader or top executive.

"An innovation, to be effective, has to be simple and it has to be focused. It should only do one thing, otherwise, it confuses. If it is not simple, it won't work. Everything new runs into trouble; if complicated, it cannot be repaired or fixed. All effective innovations are breathtakingly simple. Indeed, the greatest praise an innovation can receive is for people to say: 'This is obvious. Why didn't I think of it?' Even the innovation that creates new uses and new markets should be directed toward a specific, clearly designed application. It should be focused on a specific need that it satisfies, on a specific end result that it produces."

What he was saying was to not completely reinvent the wheel, but if you can improve the quality of the wheel, or the durability, or the price of manufacturing the wheel, by making small, yet noticeable change, you will be able to create an advancement in your ability which will look like an obvious need. However, by the time your competition applies it, you will be on to your next innovation. Part of innovation is also the courage and the sensibility to know when a certain strategy is not working, you must abandon it even, if it is a program with sentimental meaning to the executive. One more thing, change should not be a one-time or two-time occurrence over the entire existence of the corporation or an institution. Change should be a constant process; however, all change should remain in synch with the mission of the organization and or the values of the board members.

A perfect example when it comes to innovation and culling of outdated or failed products is the McDonald's Restaurant chain. While the ubiquitous international fast food chain is probably not listed among any adult diners' favorites, the chain has remained for decades the most successful fast food restaurant in the world, with "Billions and Billions Served." They have fended off hundreds of rival fast-food dining establishments and family restaurants, all of whom dream of surpassing the No. 1 restaurant in the world as measured by annual revenue. To maintain their dominance over every other restaurant in the world, they are constantly innovating the food they serve and the ways they serve it. They even tweak the way they recruit and retain employees. Not only do they consistently innovate, they literally innovate every few years like clockwork. However, just as Drucker always recommended, the changes are singular in focus. As a reference, here is an example of a McDonald's innovations timeline as listed on a recent corporate website.

1940: Dick and Mac McDonald open McDonald's Bar-B-Q restaurant in San Bernardino, California. It is a typical drive-in featuring an abundant menu and car hop service.

1948: McDonald's redesigns and reopens as a self-service drive-in restaurant. The menu is reduced to nine items: hamburger, cheeseburger, soft drinks, milk, coffee, potato chips and a slice of pie. The staple of the menu is the 15-cent hamburger.

As you can see, they have narrowed their focus to the areas of strengths–the 15-cent hamburgers. They have become self-service to enhance their strength of making their fast service the fastest service.

1949: French Fries replace potato chips and Triple Thick Milkshakes is debuted on the McDonald's menu.

They are being deliberate in the new items, which are selected to enhance the hamburger, and they are both fast enough to add to the meal without adding to the service time.

1955: Ray Kroc opens his first McDonald's in Des Plaines, Illinois, on April 15 with the attention-getting red and white tiled building with the Golden Arches.

This is the innovation of both expansion (franchising) and a logo to lure more customers from the road. This is a major advancement, while maintaining the original aesthetic of a drive-through restaurant.

1956: Fred Turner, future McDonald's Chairman is hired to work as a counter man for the Des Plaines McDonald's. He would soon become the head of McDonald's Operations defining the quality, service and cleanliness that continue to this day.

This is notable, because Chairman, Ray Krok recognizes that his most talented employee is flipping burgers and he trains him and repositions him as a Top Executive. This is a classic example of putting your most talented people in places where they can do the most for the company's growth.

1961: Hamburger University opens in the basement of the Elk Grove Village, Illinois, McDonald's restaurant.

This is the innovation of making their training programs like a university program. It instills uniformity and pride in the corporation. It also insures that every restaurant is on the same page in approach to menu and service.

1965: The Filet-O-Fish sandwich was the first item added to the national menu. Created by Cincinnati franchisee to help build volume in the predominately Roman Catholic community in which his store was located.

This innovation was more of a risk taken as a way to retain a level business while introducing a single item to the menu.

1968: The Big Mac is added to the national menu.

1973: The Quarter Pounder and the Quarter Pounder with Cheese are added to the menu.

These two innovations were subtle but huge, as they redefined the hamburgers that were the core of their business. They were able to create three hamburger options out of 2 types of patties, thus creating an expanded menu while not requiring any additional wait time.

1975: The Egg McMuffin, is added to the national menu.

By creating a limited breakfast menu, it expanded the hours of operation, took advantage of the emerging class of automobile commuters, and it created a boost to cups of coffee that are sold at a high profit margin for the franchise.

1983: Chicken McNuggets are introduced into all domestic U.S. restaurants.

This menu item expanded the restaurant into the emerging chicken market, as chicken was becoming more popular than beef. It, however, retained the quickness in preparation as the other meals, so it would not slow down service time.

1987: First McDonalds Playland built.

As children and mothers became the primary market for the fast food restaurant, the chain adapted by making the restaurants friendlier to their changing customer base.

1990: On January 31, the first McDonald's restaurant in Moscow opens. More than 30,000 customers were served on opening day!

This innovation represented essentially conquering the world. Not bad, for a company built on a foundation made of fifteen cent hamburgers!

1993: The world's first McCafé opens in Melbourne, Victoria, Australia.

By 1993, Starbucks Cafés had become a worldwide phenomenon that cut heavily into McDonalds demographic of mothers and children, so they added a Café menu and encouraged guests staying for longer visits. This was the time in this country when Fast Food was being shunned, so they began the slow but distinctive direction away from fast food and more to Café fare.

2002: McDonald's published its first ever Social Responsibility Report on April 15, 2002.

This again ties into the strength to accept trend changes and get ahead of them rather than fall behind them. As concerns about nutritional value began to cut into the chain's restaurant base, they began producing healthier items on their menu, while providing reports to share their findings with their customers. This was a huge risk that paid off well for the franchise.

2015: McDonald's USA launched All Day Breakfast.

Studies showed the traditional American breakfast times of 6-10am is an antiquated notion, so McDonalds accommodated by adapting a meal menu cycle that depicts the current 24-hour work cycle in the current American work force.

2017: Global McDelivery Day is celebrated on July 26 to support the global launch of McDelivery with UberEATS.

Now, McDonalds diners don't even have to visit the restaurant to have their favorite foods. It will be interesting to see how this latest innovation succeeds in the general market place, because McDonald's may find out that diners prefer a higher quality meat when they are inside their own home. If history tells us one thing though, it is that if the meal delivery program doesn't work, they will eliminate it, and almost as soon as this program ends there will be another innovation to replace it.

When you see all of the pragmatic and logical innovations that McDonalds has employed over the years, it's not surprising that they continue to maintain their dominance at the top of the restaurant food chain after more than a half century. One of the testaments to their strength at the highest levels of their corporations is when you see on the site that the corporation lists the individual managers and cooks who devised the subtle changes that become legitimate difference makers in maintaining their top position. Strong leaders embrace strong employees, and place them in positions to succeed at even greater levels. This is abundantly clear within the historic timeline of this highly successful American franchise.

Whether the top executive is General Electric's Jack Welch, New England Patriots' Bill Bellichick or McDonald's Ray Krok, the one thing they all share in common is that they deal from their strength. Welch put off international expansion so that he could only focus on his company's strengths. Bellichick is notorious for releasing players thought to be at the peak of their ability, in exchange for players thought to be unusable, and inserts them into positions taking advantage of their strengths, while ignoring their weakness and, so, keeps winning Super Bowls. Krok turns a hamburger chain into a trillion-dollar industry by making consistent, incremental innovations and alterations. All the titans of management and leadership have achieved their status because they succeed through strength.

> **Drucker's Wisdom**
>
> Innovation is treating changes to the system as opportunities for success.

CHAPTER VIII

INNOVATION

*"What do we know about innovation?
First, it has very little to do with genius.
It has very little or nothing to do with inspiration.
It is hard, systematic work. The myth is that an
owner-entrepreneur can depend on a flash of genius.
I have been working with owner-entrepreneurs
for 40 years; the ones who depend on a flash
of genius also go out like one."*
–Peter Drucker, 1992

Innovation matters in advanced societies because the knowledge environment is rapidly updating itself, and we live in a knowledge-based society. Innovation means abandoning old ways of thinking and applying the most current knowledge to fashion a better working institution. Innovation regards changes to relevant systems as potential opportunities for success. An innovation will not create change, but will emerge out of change. Innovations that recognize change successfully exploit opportunities, and corporations that innovate thrive.

Some of Drucker's wisest insights deal with the relation between change and innovation:

*"One cannot manage change.
One can only be ahead of it."*

Change is unavoidable. However, during the first half of the 20th century, executives as a rule believed that change should be shunned, or, at the very least, postponed for as long as possible. Acceptance to workplace change is more common now, and though it may cause some turmoil, it is acknowledged as an essential part of business growth. It is essential for modern organizations to embrace change and, in fact, lead change. It must be seen as a part of the job to create and lead change. Denying this, a company will likely weaken and perish. As Drucker often points out, "In a period of rapid change, the only ones who survive are the change leaders."

So, who are the change leaders? What do they provide, and how do they respond to change without leading the corporation straight into bankruptcy court? As mentioned in previous chapters, change agents are leaders with great strength and determination who see changes much as they see innovations, as opportunities. Not only does a change leader seek out change they also, more importantly, seek out the right changes. They also know how to implement them in ways that are effective for the organization, both from within and from the outside.

Any successful innovation will require the following **four tenets**:

1. Policies to make the future.
2. Systematic methods to look for and anticipate change.
3. The right way to introduce change, both within and outside the organization.
4. Policies to balance change and continuity.

Drucker emphasized seven key sources as opportunities for innovation, which are, in turn, opportunities for growth. They are found in: 1) the unexpected, 2) the incongruous, 3) process needs, 4) industry and market structures, 5) changes in demographics, 6) changes in perceptions, and, finally, 7) new knowledge or technology. There have been a few additional innovations; even within innovations, however, as of this date, most opportunities for innovation will fall, in one way or another, into one of these seven categories. But the order in which these sources are listed are in descending order of reliability and predictability.

Innovation should be considered in terms of its social or economic context rather than as compared to things technical. Often seemingly simple changes such as people migration can have huge impacts on the original purpose of a company. Demographics and populations change. Medical and nutritional advancements have extended the typical American's life by decades. Trends come and go and return again. As populations change, the needs of people change, and as the needs of people change, the companies that anticipate and stay ahead of change tend to have a higher success rate at serving the shifting demographic and economies and, in fact, thrive in it.

We are not yet able to develop any perfect innovation theories. But what we already do know is enough to say how, where, and when one looks systematically to exploit opportunities for innovation, and how to best judge their chances for success or failure. We now know enough to engage a practical form of innovation. Systematic innovation is a purposeful and organized search for change, and within the systematic analysis of the opportunities such changes might offer some opportunities for economic or social innovation.

However, you can't just open up an office for innovation. It's not that simple. A lot of work is also involved that allows a change agent to even recognize that a change is occurring that may be exploitable for company purposes. It is just as important for a change agent to comfortably stop their old way of doing things on a dime. Otherwise, you will never be able to innovate properly. Therefore, it is essential for an innovator to abandon the forms and assumptions of a yesterday.

An innovator should never hold onto the past, even if it has been a comfortable fit. In fact, a change agent frees all resources from committing to an obsolete program, especially if it is no longer contributing to the corporation's progress. As a matter of fact, it is not possible to prepare for tomorrow if you are clinging to your past. Future and past will always be at odds, and the innovator always sides with the future. Innovation will always present difficulties, and people stuck in the past and frightened of change will flare up when any bumps in the road occur. That is why innovation always demands leadership by people of high and proven ability. When subordinates have confidence in the leader of the policy of innovation, the team is more likely to accept the bumps in the road for what they are, and keep their energies focused toward entering the new era of innovation.

There are three reasons to completely abandon an institution's way of doing things. The first is because it only has a limited time remaining where the service will be effective. If that is the case, don't wait until it is completely obsolete. You have to take care of this immediately by abandoning and innovating. The second reason is that its only purpose is a tax write-off. Don't keep something obsolete just because it is saving you some tax dollars. The reason that it is saving you tax dollars in the first place is because it is an inefficient program to begin with. The third case that always calls for abandonment, and this Drucker emphasized as the most important reason, is when a product, service or market is old and declining. Don't keep it just because you already have it in place, because each extra year that you hold onto outdated knowledge, technology, products, markets or services is an extra year that you are falling behind in the transition to the modern tools or approaches needed to succeed.

Drucker pointed to the example of how General Motors unsuccessfully tried to stem the flow of profits captured by imported Japanese compact cars. Cars in the 1970s and 1980s needed to change to conform to the needs of the changing auto market, which demanded lower costs per vehicle and greater gas mileage to counteract the increasing cost of gasoline. While Ford and Chrysler successfully added lower cost, higher mileage vehicles, GM refused to reform or abandon their established brands. They continued to build large vehicles like Buick and Oldsmobile, figuring that tinkering with the price a little would keep their sales flowing. However, by the end of the 1980s, GM lost more than 20% of the American market share to the Japanese–a huge loss.

In the late 1990s, when GM finally got around to producing compact cars with their Saturn line, they had problems with labor unions, which felt that a change in assembly line production would sap their power. Old factories were kept open at the expense of the new cars, and they continued to make cars like the Oldsmobile line that appealed to a shrinking market. As a result, even though they were slightly more expensive, the Saturn line was making an impact in the American marketplace because Americans wanted buy American. Even so, Saturns didn't survive. GM went back to the old way of building large, cumbersome, low-mileage vehicles, only to lose an even larger percentage of the marketplace. By 2008, when GM shut down Saturn operations, they found themselves at the mercy of lenders and, after a torrent of controversy, successfully appealed to the federal government for a bailout that would keep them afloat. Finally, by the end of 2018, GM ceased operations at several outdated auto plants. The company ended up foregoing billions in growth and revenue, from which it is unlikely to ever recover. Once the world's largest automobile manufacturer, GM now has a new attitude.

Aside from a comfort level with abandonment, there is a correct way to implement innovative changes. The number one key to successful innovation is to exploit success. The saying *nothing succeeds like success* rings true. Jack Welch, former president of General Electric (1981-2001), famously only focused on products that would enhance the GE image and represent the best products. They abandoned programs the moment they were deemed not profitable enough or damaging to their reputation–GE prided themselves that they offered the best at everything they produced. Welch and GE exploited success, and used each success to launch each innovation. In each case, this innovation came as a result of making their best product better, rather than making their worst product mediocre. Welch correctly saw mediocre products as ultimately damaging to the company's bottom line.

Kentucky Fried Chicken is a wonderful example of using strengths for innovation. They have franchised their fast food chicken restaurants since 1964. In that time, they have rarely altered the core of their menu. Rather then add optional meal items such as hamburgers or fish sandwiches, they stay loyal to the concept of chicken as their primary product. When they do alter their menu, it applies to side orders, all of which accompany the core product, chicken.

When Americans' tastes shifted away from fried chicken due to concerns of trans fat, KFC first changed its recipe to include no trans fats. Next, they changed the company name from Kentucky Fried Chicken to KFC. Then, rather than adding burgers or vegan items to their menu, they added grilled chicken items–a revolutionary move. As China was beginning to open up to Western culture, KFC was the first company to take advantage of the new market, literally becoming a ubiquitous presence in China. These days, KFC is the largest American restaurant by revenue share in China, with more than 6,000 restaurants. Their final step was again exploiting their strength of brand recognition by bringing back their iconic owner turned figurehead, Colonel Harland Sanders (portrayed in his recognizable costume by animation or celebrities.)

By exploiting its strengths (chicken, Col. Sanders icons, understanding of international franchising) and by not being afraid of abandoning the term "fried" (using high trans-fat oils like palm oil) KFC has become the second largest franchise restaurant in the world with more than 20,000 restaurants and annual revenues in the tens of billions! Without having the courage to first abandon and then innovate their programs and their approaches to running, promoting and franchising their restaurants, they would likely have never expanded beyond a regional American chain, let alone continuously to expand their markets and revenues.

One area that offers the greatest opportunities for successful innovation is the unexpected success. It is already proven to be successful. It appears during a consistent flow of hard work, but then it makes everything more efficient, almost without even noticing it. Unexpected opportunities are the lowest risk opportunities for innovation. On top of that, the pursuit will be far less arduous. Yet, it is amazing how often unexpected success is completely neglected; worse, managements who fear abandoning the obsolete will work actively to reject it.

The unexpected success often challenges the longstanding judgement of higher management. More often than not, however, the unexpected success is never even noticed. Nobody pays any attention to it. The people reading the data don't even acknowledge the change in the sales chart. They assume it is a mistake on their customers' parts. Thus, the company fails to properly identify it, with the inevitable result that the competitor who runs with it reaps the rewards. Systematic innovation is necessary to prevent these golden opportunities from slipping away unexploited. Opportunities lost without ever being noticed never return. So that means that executives must set specific meetings in which to discuss unexpected successes. Furthermore, someone should be assigned to analyze any unexpected success and then figure out opportunities so that it can be exploited.

Not only is unexpected success an innovation opportunity; it demands innovation. It demands that we ask what kinds of simple changes are suddenly appropriate for this organization in how it defines its business, its technology, its markets. Whenever we consider these questions, the unexpected success is likely to open up the most rewarding and least risky of all innovative opportunities.

It's worth noting that while failure is an awful feeling, it's not the end of the world. Although failure does not go unnoticed and can often cost jobs, it can also be an impetus for change which provides opportunity. It can also be an opportunity to focus more closely on your strengths as an opportunity. Excellent executives always find opportunities in their failures as well as their successes.

Another form of an opportunity for innovation is a process need. In innovations that are based on process needs, everyone in the organization always knows that the need exists. Yet usually no one does anything about it. However, after the innovation begins, it is immediately appreciated as obvious, and shortly after, becomes standard. These are the sorts of innovations that often go unnoticed by executives; however, they are still opportunities that should not be ignored.

Drucker isolated process needs into **five specific categories**, with the caveat that the need should be clearly understood:

1. A self-contained process;
2. One "weak" or "missing" link;
3. A clear definition of the objective;
4. That the specifications for the solution can be clearly defined;
5. Widespread realization that "there ought to be a better way," that is, high receptivity.

Another opportunity for change is when industry and market structures change. This could be in the form of an economic depression or even by a natural phenomenon. In instances like the automobile industry or the 21st century dot-com bubble, industry expands and evolves so fast that innovations become obsolete almost as quickly as they are adopted. In seismically shifting markets, however, there are always plenty of available opportunities.

To outsiders, changes within industry structures offer clearly visible and predictable opportunities. To the majority of insiders, however, these same changes can be perceived as threats. The outsiders can innovate rather quickly and at relatively low risk and can thus be a major factor in an important industry or area of expertise. It's like being under and above a radar at the same time.

While the previously mentioned sources of opportunity may be internal, three sources of opportunity remain external: 1) demographics; 2) changes in perception, meaning, and mood; and finally, 3) new knowledge. Individuals change, broad populations change, certain groups migrate from East Coast to West Coast or from cities to suburbs. These changes all create opportunities to be exploited for innovation, and these are things that keen executives are mindful of.

Remember, an executive who keeps their focus on opportunities to innovate is actually seeking opportunities to strengthen the corporation and to find ways to exploit opportunities that can take areas of strength to broaden and incorporate. Do not fear abandoning things that have not worked or have outgrown their purpose. Holding onto things that have outlived their purpose will prevent the company from moving on to new programs that will advance them. Even if there is an old attachment to a program or a tax write-off, it is not worth writing off the opportunity to innovate and to exploit the available opportunities.

Once those opportunities are made available, an effective executive will exploit them. Managers will often be the sources of these innovations, and, if a company is able to, they should assign a manager to focus on innovation and ways to exploit them. The executives who lead the way to innovation tend to lead the companies which subsequently lead their business categories. That is not by coincidence. An effective executive always seeks out innovation and recognizes it and capitalizes on it when the opportunity presents itself.

Organization effectiveness is the efficiency with which an organization, group, or company is able to meet its goals. How an organization produces its set quota of products, how much waste it produces, or how efficient its processes fall under organizational effectiveness. Organizational effectiveness is about each individual from top management to subordinates performing effectively to do everything in their power to produce the desired results with a minimum expenditure of energy, time, money, and human and material resources.

Highly effective organizations exhibit strengths across **five areas**:
- Leadership
- Decision making and structure
- People
- Work processes
- Systems and culture

For an organization to achieve and sustain long term success, it requires the aptitude to adapt to its dynamic environment. Evaluating and improving organizational effectiveness and efficiency is one winning strategy used to help insure the continued growth and development of a company.

> **Drucker's Wisdom**
>
> Executives who excel understand that people don't start out seeking facts. Most fact finders begin with an opinion.

CHAPTER IX

DECISIONMAKING

"Whenever you see a successful business, someone once made a courageous decision."
–Peter Drucker

As seen in the previous chapters, a lot of preparation goes into running a corporation effectively, but if there is one distinction that an effective leader can possess, it is the knowledge and ability to make correct decisions. While the outcome of executive decisions may vary, top executives always make the final decision, and the best ones are correct more times than not. How one makes correct decisions is something that can't be learned in a book or an MBA class. The only way to learn effective decision making is by hard, consistent work and an ability to fairly evaluate the success and failure of your decision making.

Decision making is the most important, but only one of several tasks that an executive is responsible for. Decisions may take a mere nanosecond; however, each decision may have long-term effects that develop over decades, if not centuries. Making final decisions is the primary task of the top executives. The buck stops with the top executive. You can't define a top executive without discussing the importance of decision making, and what goes into that process. As Drucker would say, "Effective executives make effective decisions."

A decision is a judgment, a choice between alternatives. Typically, it is rarely a simple choice between obviously right and clearly wrong. At best, one may be able to choose between "almost right" and "almost wrong." More often than not, one's final decision will weigh the merits of competing courses of action without guarantee that one is superior to another.

Top executives are forced to make final decisions from their earliest time with a company to the last days as CEO. Top executives need to recruit their team, their staff, their fellow executives, managers and hourly employees. They have to make final decisions on their mission. They decide what product to sell–be it a tangible, manufactured product or a spiritual one offered by a church or a nonprofit organization. Even the decision to step down as CEO can be a major decision affecting jobs, revenue and the future direction of a company. So, what are the ways to make effective decisions?

Effective executives make their decisions by first observing opinions of their customers and their employees, as well as fellow managers, executives and trusted outside observers. Then, the executive reviews the facts and checks out the reliability of the data. Are the opinions in accord with the data? Do they match the expectations laid out in your action plan? Is there a necessity for an immediate change of course? To determine what is a fact requires first a decision on the criteria of relevance, and, especially, what type of measurement would be most appropriate to use. Because it is also typically the most controversial part of the decision making process, this can be the trap door for top executives.

Effective decision making doesn't stem entirely from a consensus of factual data. Drucker believed that "the understanding that underlies the right decision grows out of the clash and conflict of divergent opinions and out of the serious consideration of competing alternatives." The best decision makers take a look at the facts; however, they always consider alternatives. They aren't concrete, yet neither do they entirely dismiss the facts. Facts, by their nature, appear concrete and value-free, but opinions can lead to a stronger foundation and, additionally, create opportunities for future innovations, which in turn help organizations grow.

Executives who excel understand that most people don't start out by seeking facts. Most fact finders begin with an opinion. This is a perfectly acceptable place for any executive or manager to begin with. People experienced in an area should be expected to have an opinion. For, not having an opinion after being exposed to an area for a long time would argue that this knowledge worker is not capable of his or her job, and that they are likely either dull or lazy to boot. To not have an opinion suggests an expert who is disinterested in their job. In fact, it is literally impossible to be an effective knowledge worker, let alone an effective leader, without having knowledgeable opinions.

The top executives, the ones Drucker would classify as effective, do not focus on myriad decisions. They spend most of their energies on the one or two most important decisions. They have experts in place to handle smaller decisions, which play a part in the bigger decisions made by the top executive. Effective executives focus on broad strategic and generic issues, rather than worrying about solving small problems. They should only select the highest level important decisions in the areas of conceptual understanding. They consider the manipulation of too many variables a symptom of sloppy thinking. They want to know what the decision is all about and what the underlying realities are that it needs to satisfy. They want impact rather than approach, they want to get the job done correctly rather than in some flashy sort of way.

The highest level of efficient executives knows when a decision has to be based on principle and when it needs to be made pragmatically or merit based. They are aware that the riskiest decisions are often those in which you ultimately select between subtleties which define the correct decision and the wrong compromise and they have the experience and knowledge to be able to recognize one from the other. They know that the most time-consuming step in the process is not making the decision but putting it into effect. Unless a decision has actually evolved into an active work process, it is not a decision; it is what Drucker would describe as "at best, a good intention." This means that, while efficient decision making itself is based on the highest level of conceptual understanding, the action to proceed with these decisions should be as simple as possible and as close as possible to the working level.

Decisions that affect an entire corporation or organization should be broken down into language that those on the assembly lines or on the sales floors or in the front lines of a nonprofit can understand. It goes back to the principle of communicating the intentions in a way that employees understand, so they can all rally behind the changes. This will lead to more effective implementation of the new strategies or the new direction of production. Success or failure within decision making can be the difference between a thriving company and a failing company.

Decisions are the ultimate utilization of an executive's strength. All decisions should therefor come from a position of strength. A top executive must be strong with their presentation. They must be distinct in drawing from the strengths of the organization they are fronting. Any decisions they make should be able to take advantage of these strengths and make them stronger. Utilize the opportunity to make innovation, which should create further opportunity to improve the company's fortunes in the future. Do not focus on problems when decision making. All final decisions should strictly come with the intention of building off existing strengths.

Drucker had great admiration for Theodore Vail, CEO of Bell Telephone Systems (1885-89; 1907-1919) when it was a monopoly from the late 19th century to the first decades of the 20th century. Vail knew how to lead innovations into the future. He understood that future issues would open opportunities for innovation. He needed to compete with himself in order to stay ahead of the innovation curve and maintain his grip as the No. 1 provider of private telecommunications. Vail's programs were so successful that only the U.S. Government was eventually able to unseat him from atop the communications kingdom. That is the mark of an excellent executive.

Vail was intuitive enough to recognize that despite leading the ultimate indomitable monopoly in telecommunications, it was the most vital of all-American technical industries. He realized the value behind the notion of challenging oneself, especially while leading the industry. He recognized that the best way to maintain top performance was to challenge the company when they were in their highest position of strength. Top executives make decisions to further their company's dominance, not to maintain it. Vail recognized that the future lies in better and different technologies. The Bell Laboratories which grew out of this insight dominated telecommunications for the remainder of the century until anti-trust legislation broke it up. Drucker pinpointed this decisive innovation as the first industrial research institution that was deliberately designed to make the present obsolete, no matter how profitable and efficient. Drucker marveled,

"When Bell Labs took its final form, during the World War I period, it was a breath-taking innovation in industry. Even today, few businessmen understand that research, to be productive, has to be a 'disorganizer,' the creator of a different future and the enemy of today. In most industrial laboratories, 'defensive research' aimed at perpetuating today, predominates. But from the very beginning, Bell Labs shunned defensive research."

Defensive research is a waste of money because by definition it focuses on problems rather than strengths. Executives who base their decision making on preventing problems or focusing on plugging holes are missing out on the big picture. Making decisions with an eye on the future allows you to discard the entire problem altogether and, instead, focus on gaining a greater share or expanding the size of your market. Focusing top executive energy on an organization's problems is a surefire way to guarantee that your company will be overwhelmed by them at a later date. Make decisions that strengthen the strongest fabrics within the core of your company.

Important business decisions that are effective often have distinctive similarities, even if these decisions deal with completely different sets of problems so they lead to explicitly specific solutions. They must all confront barriers to success at the highest conceptual levels of understanding. They must work through the point of each decision, and then develop principled approaches for dealing with it. Their decisions must always be aggressive and strategic, rather than adaptations to the apparent needs of the moment. They all stay ahead of the innovation curve, with an eye on progress and building from strengths. They were often extremely controversial. Often, the boldest decisions run directly counter to what everyone, including the "experts," believes to be the only possible one at the time. The only thing that top decision makers focus on is strengthening their organization or corporation.

Drucker, as usual, was able to break the elements of excellent decision making into five steps:
1. realizing clearly that the problem is generic and can only be solved through a decision which establishes a rule, a principle;
2. defining the "boundary conditions," *i.e.*, the specifications needed to satisfy the solution to the problem

3. thinking through what is "right," that is, the solution which will fully satisfy the specifications before the elements of decision making attention are given to the compromises, adaptations, and concessions needed to make the decision acceptable;
4. building into the decision an action to carry it out; and
5. testing the "feedback" for validity and effectiveness.

An effective decision maker should self-impose a systematic review one and two years after a new decision is acted upon. The executive should rely on quality, organized information for the feedback. This feedback should contain both reports and figures. However, a truly confident and competent decision maker should always build one's feedback around direct exposure to reality. Unless an executive decision maker disciplines one's self to go out and look, they are fated to a sterile dogmatism and, with it, to ineffectiveness.

The efficient executive will make strong decisions and stand by them. Do not focus on problems, but distribute all your available resources toward fortifying areas of strength. Keep an eye on the future and compete with yourself if another organization is unable to keep up with you. Always grow your areas of strength. Review your decisions and review and revise as necessary. Only focus on one or two decisions at a time. Do not waste time worrying about the little things. Top executives understand the why, when and how of strong decision making and lead the organizations to thrive best. The highest levels of success are never there by coincidence. They are in positions of dominance due to their understanding of decision making, so that they are always in the best position to make the best decisions for their organization's continued success.

Functions of Management

Planning

Planning is the starting point and the basic primary function of management which includes formulation of one or more detailed plans to achieve optimum results or demands. It is a dynamic process and very essential for every organization to achieve their ultimate goals. It involves defining a goal and determining the most effective course of action required to reach that specific goal.

Organizing

An organization can only perform well if it is well organized. This means there must be sufficient capital, staff and raw materials so that the organization can run smoothly and efficiently. The organizational structure with a good division of functions and tasks is of crucial importance. The organizing function is an important role of the five functions of management. It is a function in which the synchronization and combination of human, physical and financial resources takes place. All the three resources are important to obtain results.

Staffing

Manning the organizational structure and keeping it staffed and operating smoothly has assumed greater importance in the recent years due to the advancement of technology, increase in size of business, and complexity of human behavior. The function of staffing and retaining a suitable workforce involves the process of recruiting, training, developing, compensating and evaluating employees, and maintaining this workforce with proper incentives and motivations. The human element is the most vital factor in the process of management.

Directing

The directing function is a key management function that includes all those activities which are designed to encourage the employees to work effectively and efficiently. It consists of process or technique by which instructions are issued and operations are carried out as originally planned. Directing is said to be the heart and soul of the management process. Planning and organizing have little importance if the directing function is not a viable component in the organization.

Controlling

The coordinating function of the management process ensures unification, integration, harmonization of the efforts of the organizational process so as to provide unity of action in pursuit of common goals. It is a hidden force which binds all the other functions of management. Management through coordinating function achieves harmony, rhythm and unity in the individual's efforts for the achievement of organizational goals.

> **Drucker's Wisdom**
>
> The best way to predict the future
> is to create it.

CHAPTER X

INTO THE FUTURE

> *"I consider myself a "social ecologist," concerned with man's man-made environment the way the natural ecologist studies the biological environment... the discipline itself boasts an old and distinguished lineage. Its greatest document is Alexis de Tocqueville's Democracy in America. But no one is as close to me in temperament, concepts, and approach as the mid-Victorian Englishman Walter Bagehot. Living in an age of great social change as I have, Bagehot first saw the emergence of new institutions: civil service and cabinet government as cores of a functioning democracy, and banking as the center of a functioning economy. A hundred years after Bagehot, I was first to identify management as the new social institution of the emerging society of organizations and, a little later, to spot the emergence of knowledge as the new central resource, and knowledge workers as the new ruling class of a society that is not only "post-industrial" but post-socialist and, increasingly, post-capitalist. As it had been for Bagehot, for me, too, the tension between the need for continuity and the need for innovation and change was central to society and civilization."*
> **–Peter F. Drucker**

Peter Drucker once famously said that, "The way to predict the future was to create it." He essentially did that by creating what is now commonly called business management. However, before he introduced his new methods of capitalism across the board with his observations and ingenuity, Drucker quietly observed in the background. He recognized certain universal elements of leadership and the running of organizations, and turned that insight into a modern science. In fact, more than a decade after Drucker's death, many of the areas of management specialization reviewed in this book continue to be as true today as when he wrote about them.

Innovations will always keep happening. Smartphone applications were never a part of Drucker's world, yet he surely would have recognized the ingenuity and evolution of this important modern technology. Social networks and social network management would be another area that he never truly got to experience firsthand. Amazon's expansion from a start up in Jeff Bezos's garage to the No. 1 form of internet retail challenging Walmart's dominance in the marketplace is an event that would have captured and inspired Drucker's imagination. Still, many of Drucker's core beliefs remain sound and practical today.

Human Relations will always count as a crucial element in managing an organization. Every executive's first important decision will always concern the hiring of personnel. An organization must hire people in top executive positions whose strengths dovetail with the primary strengths of the chief executive. They need to know what types of positions need to be filled right away to go on to tackle a company's mission and vision.

This will not change in the 21st century. The biggest changes in this regard will be to the types of positions and departments under consideration. Departments such as intra-corporate communications are enormously important in a future where offices for one company can be expected to exist on multiple continents. The innovations within communications technology also make it vital that any major corporation or nonprofit have a team dedicated to managing social networks and internet marketing, as well as the internet marketspace.

Amazon, the American electronic retailer and cloud commerce company, is a perfect example of the modern corporation employing Drucker's methods into the 21st century. Amazon began as an online book dealership run out of the founder's, Jeff Bezos's, garage. By the time of Drucker's death in 2005, Amazon had already proven that online commerce was profitable and sustainable. Although he hadn't yet made 7-figure annual revenues (he was getting close and by 2007), Amazon employed more than 15,000 people worldwide.

One of their great innovations was by paying attention to the sorts of employees they hired. They made sure to only bring on board new hires who were excited about online retailing with an eye toward the future and with a literacy of all things internet. By hiring experts in placing content where people can see it, they revolutionized search engine optimization. Bezos was forward thinking enough to realize that not only does he have to create a space on the internet where he can sell his wares (which at the time was primarily books), he also had to create ways to locate his online storefront for his current and future customers. By hiring employees who were specifically ahead of the curve in internet and online retailing, he was able to forge a team of knowledge experts who not only were not intimidated by innovation but actually thrived on it.

Communications will be essential in the 21st century and Drucker's theories are already proving true in these instances as well. Amazon is the obvious example again, as they will often be in the 21st century. They have surpassed Walmart as the pinnacle of American consumer revenue. They are ubiquitous on the Internet and are at the vanguard of online surveys. The customer ratings system, which singles out reputable dealers from less reputable ones, is among their primary innovations in the field of effective communications. This gives a voice to the customers, who then, in turn, provide assurances for future customers about which books to buy, and from which third party dealers on the system to purchase. These innovations aren't earthshaking. Five-star systems have been used for decades in entertainment, and a scale of 1 to 10 has been used for everything from physical pain to academic rating. However, by making it a feature of internet commerce, Amazon effectively removed the boogieman factor of anonymity, successfully turning mysterious unknown online retailers into a marketing tool for managing sales with customers' expectations.

Nonprofits will remain the No. 1 employer in America into the 21st century. Drucker correctly identified the need for second careers, as well as a life away from home and office. By following a spiritual path for a few hours a week, in conjunction with your primary career, you will not only satisfy other parts of your human interests, you will also be more effective at combatting burnout. In the 21st century, this is evident as you see many successful dot com millionaires and billionaires segueing into various capacities in nonprofits. Nonprofits rely on the energy of a volunteer workforce, and they have several different groups that need focusing on at the same time. They do not rely on cash revenues as much as they do on human fulfillment. However, cash revenues are still required to operate at the highest levels. The nonprofit is an ever-evolving field, and, as evident during the times of a non-charitable administration like that of president Donald J. Trump, diminished cash flow can often mean the last gasp from distressed to destroyed. This will become abundantly evident during the next decade, when nonprofits that run like healthy for-profit corporations will be the organizations which experience the most success with their respective missions.

Effective leaders will always have a seat at the table in the executive suite. Top leaders will always have to make the most crucial decisions, and they will also direct the organization's success. An excellent leader will have the vision and the courage to steer the corporate ship in the fastest direction, and those companies with weak leadership will constantly question themselves and ultimately perish. The top leaders in the 21st century will have to focus on the same area that the effective leaders in the 20th century focused on, namely innovation, decision making, pouncing on opportunities and improving areas where the company is already strong.

Even in the future, when companies fail to operate from positions of strength, they can slip from the top of their market. In the 21st century, you can see countless variations of the same story. A company tries to stem the tide of losses in an area that could just as easily be completely eliminated. Meanwhile, as they lose focus of what worked for them in the past, another company that previously held the No. 2 or No. 3 position may overtake them. That is not to say that a company should never expand into new areas, but they should only expand into areas if they tie into the long-term vision of the company.

Drucker's lessons on mergers and acquisitions are extremely influential in the 21st century, even more so than in the 20th Century.

1. Acquire a company with a 'common core of unity'– either a common technology or market or, in some situations, production processes. Financial ties alone are insufficient.
2. Think through your firm's potential contributions of skills to the acquired company. There must be a contribution and it has to be more than money.
3. Respect the products, markets and customers of the acquired company. There must be a 'temperamental fit'.
4. Within the first year of a merger, a large number of managers of both companies should receive substantial promotions from one of the former

companies to the other. You are not buying the management. The management does not have to be replaced at the acquired company. However, there should be an official hierarchy in place, including a manager or executive from the acquiring company to oversee their new acquisition and ensure that the company contributes to the growth of the acquiring company.
5. Within the first year of a merger, a large number of managers of both companies should receive substantial promotions from one of the former companies to the other.

It will be essential in the era of mergers and acquisitions for the absorbed companies to continue producing and integrating seamlessly into the acquiring company. Everyone needs to be on the same page. This is why it is essential to make acquisitions where it makes sense. Everybody needs to speak the same language, so the companies can combine seamlessly. It's even more important when the acquisitions occur on an international level, because you will not only be dealing with a different corporate culture, you will be dealing with a different social environment as well.

Drucker's influence will continue for decades and, likely, for centuries. In 1987, Claremont Graduate University's management school was named the Peter F. Drucker Graduate School of Management in his honor. His archives are routinely viewed online. In those archives, he catalogued interviews and observations from decades of working with the most elite of all-American business executives covering a period of time extending over a century. From pioneering automobile executives like General Motors CEO Alfred Sloan to 21st century future executives, the Drucker management tree goes beyond mere branches, it extends to a vast forest.

Drucker's books have been reprinted dozens of times now, and it is hard to find an MBA graduate not familiar with Drucker's approach to business management. Many self-made executives and entrepreneurs apply his methods without even being aware of it. Even sports figures like Bill Belichick and Robert Kraft, owner of the New England Patriots, applies Drucker's philosophies to great success. In fact, whenever you see someone succeeding at the highest levels, they are likely benefitting from Drucker's philosophies, as many self-help books take cues from his early work on self-assessment and self-awareness. His influence permeates all forms of media. He established the Drucker Archives at Claremont Graduate University in 1999; the Archives became the Drucker Institute in 2006. It wasn't until 2002, at age 92, that Drucker finally retired from the classroom. He continued consulting businesses and nonprofit organizations well into his nineties.

Drucker's insightful catchphrase, "Do what you do best and outsource the rest" although sometimes controversial has become a standard practice over time. In today's era of international trade, combining technical innovations of fiber optics, Skype video, Dropbox, and email culture, it is possible for organizations to operate round the clock. Large corporations outsource jobs to knowledge workers in far flung regions of the world, where, due to the U.S. dollar exchange rate, workers can fill positions at considerable savings to the company. Many international companies will send one or two representative managers to oversee operations–another Drucker philosophy. These days, the outsourcing philosophy has been co-opted, and some would say exploited by outsourcing minimum-wage and low-wage data entry jobs to overseas countries with drastically reduced wages. This was never Drucker's intention when he endorsed outsourcing, and this is more of a cost-cutting decision. However, with the proliferation of education around the world these days, the supply and demand of the market creates an opportunity to cut costs with high-level knowledge workers at relatively low wages. It would be irresponsible for an effective top executive to pass up the opportunity, especially if it allowed the company to expand its market.

Drucker was the first business consultant to recognize the workers' humanity and emphasized respect for workers, not as a union supporter, but as an advocate of effective management. In the balance, Drucker never considered employees to be liabilities, but rather a company's greatest assets. He professed that knowledgeable workers are the essential ingredients of the modern economy, and that a hybrid management model that highlights the strengths of individual employees and places them in positions to succeed is the sole method of demonstrating an employee's value to an organization. Central to his philosophy is that the human factor is an organization's most valuable resource, and the manager is responsible for both preparing people to perform and giving them leeway to do so. These methods will continue to apply well into the 21st century.

Drucker's belief that effectiveness must be learned and earned is always going to be the ultimate statement of an executive's effectiveness. There will always be companies who hand down the responsibility of running the company to blood relatives, but in those cases, the departing top executive has to do everything in their power to make sure that their replacement is entirely prepared, not just to take over leading the company, but to lead the company for the foreseeable future.

Leaders and top executives will always have to keep an eye open for opportunities to innovate, because innovation will always be the primary sources of strength. Apple Inc. compared to former leader of the computer market, IBM, presents a perfect example of how two companies dealt with opportunities for innovation. IBM resisted change. They were slow to abandon their approach to promotion, innovation and sales. Their products were behind the curve when it came time to innovate, so each time innovation in their industry occurred, they ceded a larger portion of the market pie. When the trend was heading in the direction of retail personal computers, IBM ceded the market to Apple. The same results occurred when Apple created laptops and computers that were easier for regular people to use. When laptops became commonplace, Apple turned their focus toward expanding their strengths, sleekness, "cool factor" and ease of use, and they were able to expand into the music industry with i-Pods and Apple music, and telephones with the i-Phones. Each innovation expanded Apples' market share until they dominated their market sector, along with telecommunications and music, which all ran through their core product, their computers. They continue to innovate with the expansion of the Apple Stores, which is literally an Apple storefront. It is a revolutionary approach and continues to propel their sales and further strengthen the company as a whole.

Peter Drucker passed way in 2005 at the age of 95. To his final days, he continued advocating for advancements in business management and the efficient running of non-profits. His decades of work as a professor, an author, an innovator and the literal father of business management blazed a path to help future business executives learn how to be effective. His lessons will open the eyes of brighter executives both in corporations and non-profits. Peter Drucker's philosophies and his lessons are a roadmap for success and his impact will be felt for decades to come. Every effective executive bears the stamp of Peter Drucker's lessons.

CHAPTER SUMMARIES

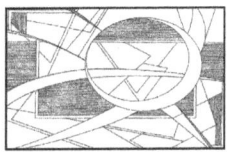

CHAPTER I: **Self Awareness**

Five Decision Steps:
1. Think carefully through the work assignment.
2. Look at several qualified people and your options to match the job description.
3. Always study the performance record of candidates.
4. A person in charge of making people decisions should reach out to people who have worked for them before.
5. Always make sure that the new manager knows exactly how success is to measured.

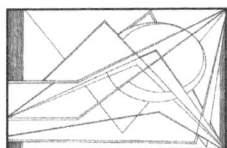

CHAPTER II: **Human Relations and People**

- Successful management is the belief that with self-control and self-management one can rise to the top of their chosen profession.
- A person can perform only from strengths. One cannot build performance on weakness.
- Feedback analysis is a simple but vital step to discovering both your strengths and weaknesses as an executive manager.
- Based on learning style and approach to success, the goal is to place yourself in the best situation for your optimum success.

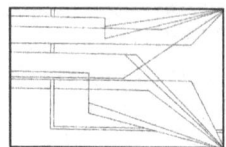

CHAPTER III: **Communicating Correctly**

Four Fundamentals of Communication:
1. Perception
2. Expectation
3. Demands
4. Communication and Information

- Communication is the most important element in business management.
- Drucker quoted Plato: *"One must speak in the language of the recipient experience"*.
- Communication makes demands. It always appeals to motivation for someone to do something or believe something.
- A top executive in communicating, must ask themselves what they can do to help their staff achieve the company's goals.

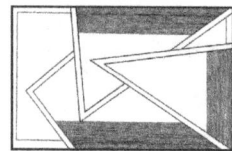

CHAPTER IV: **Self-Assessment**

- Assess what you are doing as a company, why you are doing it, and what you need to do as a company to meet overall performance.
- Mission does not need to be specific, but has to direct you towards what you hope to accomplish.
- Successful leadership anticipates the future and adapts to it.
- A smart organization keeps vigilance over who their primary and secondary customers are.
- Seek out what your customers want.

CHAPTER V: **Nonprofits–Mission to Performance**

- Nonprofits need special attention because of the absence of a traditional bottom line. Their mission is less about dollars and more about improving quality of life.
- Drucker approached the philanthropic nature of nonprofit organizations as a for-profit business world.
- Nonprofits sell the moral conscience that allows ordinary people to look in the mirror and see the best version of themselves.
- The nonprofit encourages the philanthropist to read the literature provided and the donors begin to identify.
- The organization benefits from the free labor, which will ideally push the group to exceed their goals.

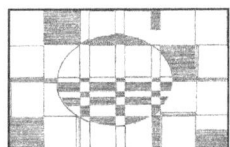

CHAPTER VI: **Leadership**

Drucker's Eight leadership practices:
1. Ask what needs to be done
2. Ask what is right for the firm
3. Develop action plan
4. Responsibility for the decision
5. Responsibility for communication
6. Focus on opportunities rather than problems
7. Productive meetings
8. Express need in terms of "we" rather than "I"

- An effective action plan
- Intolerant to underachievement
- Management skills: conceptual, human and technical
- Innovation is an important key for future success

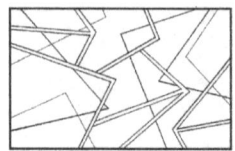

CHAPTER VII: Success Through Strength

- Effective leaders need to lead through strength
- An effective top executive will recognize the strengths of each staff member they hire and they will be placed in a position to develop their strengths to their fullest capacity
- A human excels in relating perception to action and works best if the entire person, muscles, senses and mind is engaged by the work.
- Strong leaders don't worry about whether they are liked or not. They concern themselves with whether or not the employee is properly completing assigned work.
- Innovation is an important asset to companies that rely on strength for success.

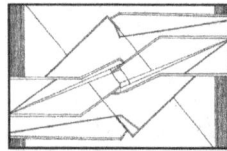

CHAPTER VIII: Innovation

Four Tenets of Successful Innovation:
1. Policies to make the future
2. Systematic methods
3. Effective introduction to change
4. Policies to balance change and continuity

- Innovation means abandoning old ways of thinking and applying the most current knowledge.
- It is essential for modern organizations to embrace change and lead change.
- As populations change, the needs of the people change. The companies that anticipate and stay ahead of change tend to have a higher success rate.
- Innovation always demands leadership by people of high and proven ability. Confidence in the leader of innovative policies inspires the team to keep their energies focused toward the new era.

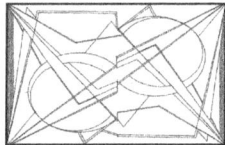

CHAPTER IX: **Decision Making**

- Decision making is the most important role of the executive because it can have long term effects.
- Executives make their decisions by first observing opinions of their customers, employees, and other managers.
- Effective executives focus on broad strategic and general issues
- Drucker's elements of excellent decision making
- The highest levels of success are never there by coincidence. Positions of dominance are due to understanding decision making.

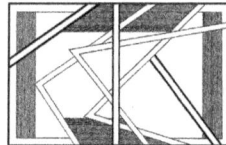

CHAPTER X: **Into the Future**

- Drucker recognized certain universal elements of leadership and the running of organizations, and turned that insight into a modern science.
- The innovations within communications technology also make it vital that any major corporation or nonprofit have a team dedicated to managing social networks and internet marketing.
- The consumer ratings system which singles out reputable dealers from less reputable ones, is among the primary innovations in the field of effective communications.
- Everyone needs to speak the same language.
- The human factor is an organization's most valuable resource.

APPENDIX I

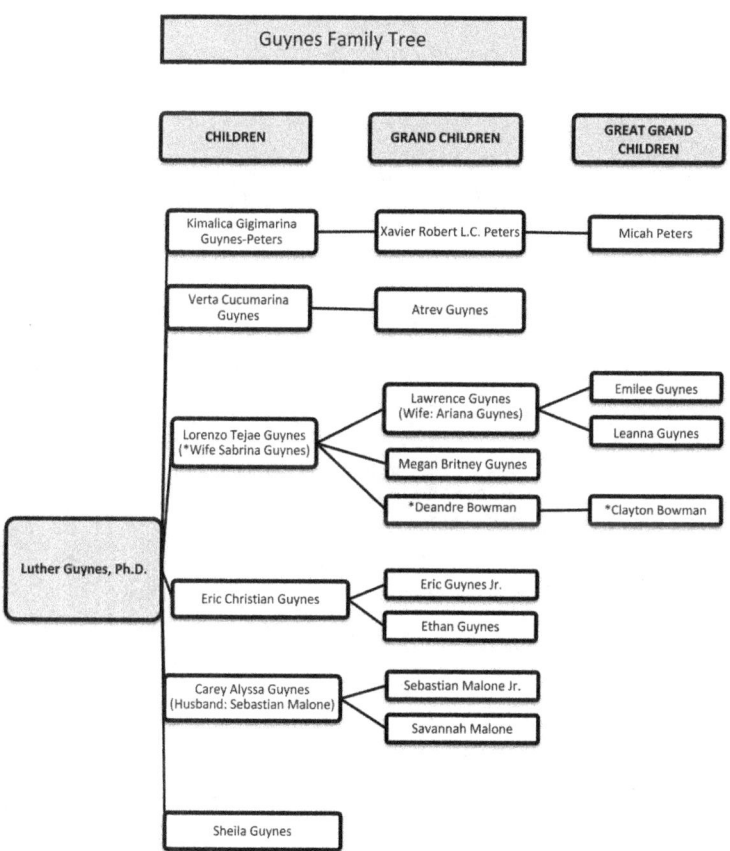